What Your Colleagues Are Saying . . .

The enduring contribution of this book is in the guidance it provides leaders to recognize that they are part, an important part, but just a part, of a networked system. As such, their decisions and actions send messages throughout the system about what is valued and what is not. Take heed of McDowell's advice and you'll have a healthy, growth-producing system that will be the envy of those around you. The work is possible, the information is available, and the results are clear.

—Douglas Fisher, Professor of Educational Leadership
San Diego State University

As the rules governing the practice of education evolve, educational leaders must be at the forefront of learning to be able to lead effectively. Through my experience in research and professional development, and as a school district administrator, I know firsthand that the evolution of any practice—including education—must be informed by those on the front line who are thought-leader practitioners. In his book, The Lead Learner, *Dr. McDowell, provides a case for why it is important for the leaders of learning organizations to continue their learning and to be at the forefront of discovery. He provides practical examples though empirical research and storytelling of ways that educational leaders can achieve the status of the lead learner.*

—Bernadine Futrell, Director, Leadership Services
AASA, The School Superintendents Association

It is great to pick up a book that puts learning first. This book offers an elegant set of resources that make leading learning so much easier. This is an essential resource for practicing and aspirant school leaders.

—Neil MacNeill, Head Master
Ellenbrook, Western Australia

These tools, ideas, and resources will help you develop a shared commitment to improved learning for all. This book builds upon the work of respected researchers and practitioners, with the goal of achieving the outcomes that are most essential for ALL students.

—Lynn Macan, Visiting Assistant Professor
University at Albany, SUNY

The Lead Learner

Improving Clarity, Coherence, and Capacity for All

Michael McDowell

Foreword by Douglas Fisher
Epilogue by Peter M. DeWitt

CORWIN
A SAGE Publishing Company

FOR INFORMATION:

Corwin

A SAGE Company

2455 Teller Road

Thousand Oaks, California 91320

(800) 233-9936

www.corwin.com

SAGE Publications Ltd.

1 Oliver's Yard

55 City Road

London EC1Y 1SP

United Kingdom

SAGE Publications India Pvt. Ltd.

B 1/I 1 Mohan Cooperative Industrial Area

Mathura Road, New Delhi 110 044

India

SAGE Publications Asia-Pacific Pte. Ltd.

3 Church Street

#10-04 Samsung Hub

Singapore 049483

Publisher: Arnis Burvikovs

Development Editor: Desirée A. Bartlett

Editorial Assistant: Eliza Erickson

Production Editor: Amy Schroller

Copy Editor: Terri Lee Paulsen

Typesetter: C&M Digitals (P) Ltd.

Proofreader: Dennis W. Webb

Indexer: Judy Hunt

Cover Designer: Michael Dubowe

Marketing Manager: Nicole Franks

Printed in the United States of America

ISBN 978-1-5443-2498-2

This book is printed on acid-free paper.

Certified Chain of Custody
Promoting Sustainable Forestry
www.sfiprogram.org
SFI-01268

SFI label applies to text stock

18 19 20 21 22 10 9 8 7 6 5 4 3 2 1

Contents

Foreword

Fritjof Capra, the physicist who authored *The Tao of Physics* (1975), believes that organizations operate like organisms, networked into systems. I had the opportunity to learn directly from Capra many years ago. I had read his book *Uncommon Wisdom: Conversations With Remarkable People* (1988), in which he shares the discussions he has had with major thinkers, such as Krishnamurti, Bateson, Grof, Schumacher, and Indira Gandhi, and signed up for one of his seminars. I wanted to have a conversation with a remarkable person, one who personally knew the major contributors to ideas of our times.

During our weekend seminar, we explored the ways in which systems work together. At the time, he was developing his ideas that would become the book *The Web of Life* (1997) and was focused on systems thinking, an idea whose time had not yet come. Today, we readily use the phrase "systems thinking" and we hope to achieve that type of thinking in our work. To my thinking, when school leaders understand systems thinking, they make better decisions and the organization becomes healthier. When leaders do not understand the impact of their decisions on the system, they weaken all parts of the organization they are trying to lead.

As a quick example, I'll focus on something that happened the day before I began to write this foreword. A teacher at our school was hired, mid-year, to be a school leader in another school. This is not uncommon as our school is seen as the "farm" in which leaders are grown, and other schools (and the district office) pluck them when they are ripe and ready. We never want to hold anyone back, and we celebrate each time a person from our school is chosen to lead. But in this case, the teacher was leaving mid-year and we needed to find a replacement. One of the recommendations, from a new leader, was to offer the position to a paraprofessional we will call Sandra, who worked at the school and who was finishing her teaching credential.

This person said, "Sandra would be great because she already knows our school culture." In response, I said, "You are right. But what will happen to the college stats and trig classes that she tutors for our seniors? Who will take responsibilities for those?" The outcome of this particular decision is not relevant to this book, but the idea of systems thinking is. This is a simple example of the impact of systems thinking. There are, of course, much bigger decisions that require deep understanding of systems thinking.

Systems thinkers must have the ability to (1) conceptualize schools as complex organizations comprised of a network of dynamic and interdependent thinking components, (2) pursue school change and improvement through systemic change and capacity building, and (3) create and articulate a shared vision of a school as a place where all students are fully engaged, inspired, empowered, and their voices are heard. Systems thinkers ask:

- ❑ How do I conceptualize my organization as a system with internal and external influences?
- ❑ How do I tie *types of thinking* together to pursue school change and improvement through systemic change?
- ❑ How do I adapt my leadership when circumstances require changes in *what, why,* or *how* things need to be done?
- ❑ How does our vision to promote every student's voice drive our long-range and short-term strategic thinking and execution?
- ❑ How do I articulate and model beliefs about the value of every student's voice as a critical element to educational outcomes?

You might be asking yourself why I remembered the training with Capra after all these years or why I am writing about systems thinking. It's because Michael McDowell's book *The Lead Learner* made me. Capra is a systems thinker, but not a school systems thinker. McDowell fills that gap. In this book, McDowell articulates the components of the school system that leaders must attend to. He continually redirects readers to notice other aspects of the system that will be impacted by the decisions that are made. He begins our journey focused on clarity, asking three questions. Leaders who strive to find the answers to these three questions will understand their system in deep ways. When they do, they have the chance of positively impacting that system.

McDowell does not leave us at the questioning phase. He moves to building coherence within the system. We all have experience with schools and districts that lack coherence, despite the best efforts of leaders to create and maintain coherence. To me, a lack of systems thinking prevents coherence from taking hold. The absence of a systems thinking approach undermines efforts to maintain coherence as each decision has seemingly random impacts on other parts of the system and leaders spend their time in crisis mode, responding to one problem after another.

Following the exploration of coherence, McDowell turns his attention to capacity. And a powerful turn he takes. Building capacity in others, understanding the impact that succession planning and talent management play in an organization, is among the most important roles that the lead learner plays. Unfortunately, most of us were not taught how to do this, and some of us are afraid of it. *The Lead Learner* contains practical and useful advice, don't get me wrong. But I think that the enduring contribution of this book is in the guidance it provides leaders to recognize that they are part, an important part, but just a part, of a networked system. As such, their decisions and actions send messages throughout the system about what is valued and what is not. Take heed of McDowell's advice and you'll have a healthy, growth-producing system that will be the envy of those around you. The work is possible, the information is available, and the results are clear. It's up to you to choose to engage with the systems you lead. Enjoy.

Douglas Fisher
Professor of Educational Leadership
San Diego State University

Preface

Lead the Learning

The *greatest* impact educational leaders can have on student learning is advocating for and engaging in teacher learning and development. The act of learning with and learning from teachers as they explore, develop, and master new skills and content to influence student learning has the potential to yield well over more than one year's growth in student learning. Moreover, as Viviane Robinson (2011) has established in her work *Student-Centered Leadership*, no other leadership initiative even comes close to the effect on student learning than engaging in teacher learning and development. As such, it is important for us, as leaders, to pause and ask ourselves how much time are we willing to invest in (and lead others to build) policies, programs, and practices that focus squarely on learning?

Research shows that almost every initiative and intervention in education works (Hattie, 2009). Likewise, almost every type of leadership approach and behavior works to enhance student learning. That means that leadership actions, such as ensuring students are in class on time, enough money is being allocated to the math department, textbook review committees are scheduled, school breaks are scheduled appropriately, and teachers are evaluated per the union contract, work. That is, practices that underpin ensuring an orderly environment, strategically allocating resources, and coordinating and evaluating teaching and the curriculum are effective in improving student learning. For many school leaders these actions are why they were hired, where they spend their time, and where they default to in their decision-making and daily priorities when things get hard (which is often).

This book focuses squarely on positioning leaders to spend the majority of their day on leading the learning. These lead learners spend their time on actions that actively involve them, their staff, and students on learning. They clarify in their strategic plans specific initiatives that will directly and substantially impact student learning and will clarify what they won't spend their time, energy, and effort on. They design educational and human resource systems that ensure that the most effective impact strategies will be in place in every classroom while leveraging the best teacher and staff autonomy to make decisions that enhance their learning. They focus on continually investing in their own learning and that of their staff. They worry less about being an instructional leader or whether they are a 21st-century school or a rigorous program and more on the approaches that support the growth and proficiency of all staff and learners. They see integrity to learning being much more important than fidelity to a pacing guide, plan, or teaching practice. They transcend major debates and orient themselves to the core purpose of a learning organization: making a substantial impact on learning.

The forces against the behaviors that the lead learner uses to enhance learning are very strong. One example outside of education particularly comes to mind: Wilt Chamberlain's 1962 100-point game in Hershey, Pennsylvania. Chamberlain still holds the record for the highest score by an individual in any game, but what is less known is that his free throw percentage that night was in the high 90s—more than twice his average. Why? He used the granny shot. The granny shot is a method of shooting free throws by lowering the ball between the knees and then moving the arms toward the head and releasing the ball as one nears the chest. The method has a very high success rate but is considered unattractive and socially unacceptable by both fans and teammates. Chamberlain eventually quit using the high-impact strategy and his free throw percentage fell. Social pressure won out over effectiveness.

As a superintendent, I'm constantly rallying my staff, board, and community to focus on feedback, clarity of expectations, and enabling students to track their own progress. This is much less appealing than extolling the values of virtual reality, project-based learning, and new learning spaces. The essential granny shots I argue for each day are executed in the educational system I serve because I lead by example, infusing the idea of staying small and staying focused on investing in those practices that substantially enhance learning. I have found that I have had to take several granny shots along the way to be a lead learner, and the impact on student and staff learning has been significant and substantial, although perhaps not glamorous.

The fact that school leaders are in a position to substantially affect the greatest number of people in a given school makes them the decisive element in that school. Do we have the courage to stay put and not fly to Finland or China for the next educational silver bullet? Do we have the courage to recognize that we do not need to "catch up" to the latest PISA (Program for International Student Assessment) superpower? Do we have the courage to proudly support traditional practices that have substantially enhanced student learning over time while also embracing more recent innovations if they are substantially working with our learners? Do we have the courage to say that we will stop engaging in priorities and practices that make minimal or modest gains in student learning even when they are popular? Most importantly, do we have the courage to stop doing what works and start consistently doing what it takes to make a substantial impact on the learning of all children? This courage is necessary because as we will see, almost everything in education works. We have to focus our daily actions on what makes a substantial impact.

Let's think about our own leadership behavior over the past six weeks. What was the percentage of time we spent in our last staff meeting discussing the core cognitive principles that are key to enhancing student learning? How much time did we spend with our teachers as they were working on figuring out how to ensure students were clear on the learning targets of a lesson or unit? When was the last time we went into a classroom observation and focused squarely on the students in the classroom and not the teacher to make an informed decision on their growth in learning? When was the last time we led the learning of our staff?

Do we have the courage to focus our leadership actions on substantially enhancing the learning of all students and staff in our system? This is a book about stepping away from the default of leadership practices that work and stepping into and ushering others into focusing on leadership that goes beyond what works to what works best. You are the decisive element, and this is a book on how you and others can take the granny shot to ensure everyone is learning at high levels.

After reading this book, you will be able to

- Create a strategic plan that ensures students demonstrate substantial growth in 20th- and 21st-century knowledge and skills.
- Align teaching and learning practices to ensure students meet and exceed core outcomes across levels of complexity (surface, deep, and transfer).

- **Standardize hiring practices** that identify and select candidates that have beliefs and behaviors that will move learning forward on Day 1.
- **Build capacity** to ensure that educators develop and refine their skills to impact students' development of 20th- and 21st-century knowledge and skills.
- **Develop leadership skills** that will enable you to model best practices to move learning forward for all stakeholders.

Special Features

- **4Cs:** The four key features of a lead learner—clarity, coherence, capacity, and crafting—provide a framework for leaders to develop systems that make a substantial impact on student and teacher learning.
- **Researched-based strategies:** Each section of the book is thoroughly research based, providing multiple sources to substantiate the benefits and successful strategies of the lead learner.
- **Voices from the field:** Educators who are interested in implementation can find valuable insights from the *Voices From the Field* sections, where educational leaders reflect on their experience leading the learning in their system.
- **Activities:** These will help you create your own next steps in designing plans; aligning curriculum, instruction, and hiring practices; and developing teacher capacity and personal leadership skills.
- **Examples, tables, checklists, protocols, rubrics, and images:** These will facilitate understanding and application of the material.
- **Appendix:** This offers every protocol mentioned in the book, along with tools and examples for supporting leaders in their own practice.
- **Reflection questions:** Chapter-end reflective questions will assist you in thinking about how these strategies apply to your own leadership practices within your unique context and role.
- **Next steps:** Each chapter ends with Next Steps that encourage you to apply the content of each chapter to get you started in improving your leadership practices.

A Perspective From a Lead Learner

Transitioning all of my actions to focusing on learning has taken courage. Our work in education is so emotional. Preserving our emotional reserves to do focused work is vital. Part of my shift toward becoming a lead learner has been making conscious choices to devote that emotional energy toward developing a culture of learning and *away from* the focus toward procedural and managerial matters. I have found that it is so easy to default to procedural and managerial responsibilities as opposed to ushering in conversations focused on learning in every daily practice. I do not attempt to discount the importance of safely and efficiently running a building. However, this shift, for me, has centered on how much time and where I choose to spend energy. I have made some specific changes that have resulted in a shift toward the learning process, and our team has embarked on a collective eagerness to engage in the continuous cycle of transformation and improvement toward our goal: *at least one year of academic growth in one year's time.*

I have found that there is a push internally and externally to drift to new ideas, explore new approaches, or go back to the traditional managerial problems that keep me from anchoring my decision-making with staff that substantially impacts student learning. However, once I made the switch, everything become clear and simple (not easy) but doable to move the learning forward for every student and staff member every day.

What I learned in making the shift is that it required a "flip." We call it 90–10, meaning that 90% of our conversations revolve around learning and 10% address the procedural items. I began to identify, categorize, and monitor the time I spent on those procedural and managerial items (i.e., opening school procedures, scheduling, budgeting, transportation) because those events took me away from the conversations related to learning. The tally was astounding. It was opposite of where I wanted to be as a leader.

This took risk, courage, belief in the clarity of our direction, and most of all permission to say "no." We've all been there where we have a wonderful yearlong, aspirational plan. Then, reality happens; wildfires, lockdowns, bad press, loss of buses for transportation, revolving-door subs—each with a range of impacts that require immediate solutions. Each potentially exhausting, tapping into those emotional reserves. Contributing time and energy to the tasks, beyond the immediate necessary steps, takes away from reaching our academic goal. The decision on *what* and *how much* to focus on is a choice. When we identified that many of the procedural matters are out of our sphere of influence, we equally defined what *is* in our sphere of influence: learning.

Creating this type of direction takes courage in knowing that the direction is valuable and will lead to accelerating learning. One approach is to "model the way" by creating a manageable, transparent, yearlong plan that transcends the aspirational and includes concise essential learning intentions and success criteria with incremental checkpoints for feedback. In other words, everything we ask our teachers to do we do ourselves, first. This not only lends to credibility, but also the humbling recognition that this work is hard!

Starting small by identifying the few colleagues on site who are willing to take the risk toward the focus on learning helped tremendously. Having the structure of the yearlong plan creates opportunity to simultaneously maintain direction while conducting the action research and inquiry that brings individuality and excitement to the work. It is also accountability for the leaders, learners, and commitment toward meeting the goal. This requires being open to feedback from your colleagues, including utilizing critical friends, protocols, and feedback surveys on what's working and what's not.

One of the most concrete components to shifting the work and actually moving forward has been the use of student voice protocols. Capturing, sharing, and reflecting on what students say about the direction has been illuminating. When students articulate where they are in their own learning has really helped to define *why we are here.*

Being able to delineate between procedural times and learning time, establishing a concise yearlong plan, monitoring emotional investment, being comfortable with uncomfortable dialogue, and enacting change are a few options to begin the process toward the focus on learning.

My journey has shown me that every day I have to have the discipline to say no to things that are popular, are trendsetting, are comfortable, and instead focus on small, incremental changes that yield a substantial impact on learning. And, the results have shown a substantial impact—not just on students but teachers. I have delegated low-impact issues to others so that I may focus on the teaching and learning in my building. I don't outsource the learning of my staff—I'm in it with them, learning. I'm always modeling the learner because I am actually learning in time, with staff. This is powerful for them to see that I bring humility, confidence, optimism, and a desire to grow to the table.

This road to focusing on learning is hard. It is much easier to focus on tasks during walkthroughs than asking questions about learning. It is much easier to focus on instructional practices than it is to talk about how students are performing. It is much easier to focus on curriculum, schedules, and strategic plans than to review student performance data, co-construct the meaning of such performance, and create next steps collectively. During the course of this journey as a lead learner, I have found that I have had to let go of the "politics of distraction"—those variables that are interesting and popular to talk about but don't move the needle in learning. I have found that I have had to create a narrative to frame for others what we are going to focus on to ensure substantial growth in learning for all students and staff. I have found that small incremental changes have moved my learning forward and that of others. And, lastly, I have found that when I keep everyone focusing on a few substantially impactful practices great things happen for students and staff.

Today, the problems that come to me, the dialogues I engage in, the decision-making I'm a part of, and the priorities that I set with others are aligned directly with the growth in learning for staff, students, and myself. We are getting more than one year's growth in one year's time because we are focusing on the learning. I'll never go back—my leadership is tied to learning and my school is tied to one focus: learning for all, at high levels, and I go first.

Melissa A. Lambert, Principal
Konocti Education Center
Clearlake, California

Author's Acknowledgments

The Lead Learner is dedicated to those who have and continue to lead the learning—to those leaders who have never been satisfied with students "doing their best" or having others "do their best," but rather move them beyond what they thought they were capable of becoming.

From watching and learning from a mother, who as a single parent with three children went back to school to get a degree in math and designed a thriving tutoring program in rural Oklahoma, to the opportunity to partner with Laurie Kimbrel as we embarked on disrupting the pedagogy of privilege and the soft bigotry that can permeate classrooms, policies, and practices in schools. To the teachers and support staff at Ross School, who continue to demonstrate on a daily basis that there is tremendous expertise in education, that teachers can substantially impact learning, and that public education can transcend our own expectations on their impact on our children.

I would like to acknowledge Letty Watt, Sally Kennedy, Dr. Barbara Murray, Joanna Mitchell, Lexie Cala and many, many others who influenced the writing of this book and my leadership. To Pete Pillsbury, who fundamentally influenced my understanding of personnel; Professor John Hattie, who influenced my understanding of learning and teaching; Napa New Tech High, for changing my life; and Shirley Clarke, Kara Vargas, Sarah Martin, Sophie Murphy, Deb Howe, Doug Fisher, and Peter DeWitt for their influence on my thinking and leadership.

To my wife and children: thank you for your patience and support.

And last but not least, I want to thank Daisy, a former student of mine, who taught me the importance of always focusing on children, their lives, and their passions over teaching, and to always move children past their own expectations and for them to move us past ours. . . .

Publisher's Acknowledgments

Corwin gratefully acknowledges the contributions of the following reviewers:

Carrie Carpenter, Oregon Teacher of the Year 2003, Consultant
Redmond, Oregon

Lynn Macan, Retired Superintendent, Visiting Assistant Professor
University at Albany–SUNY
Albany, New York

Neil MacNeill, Head Master
Ellenbrook Independent Primary School
Western Australia, Australia

Lena Marie Rockwood, Assistant Principal
Revere High School
Revere, Massachusetts

Joy Rose, Retired Principal
Westerville South High School
Westerville, Ohio

About the Author

Michael McDowell, EdD, serves as the superintendent of the Ross School District. During his tenure, the Ross School District has progressed to the top of California districts in relation to student connectedness and well-being as well as being in the top tier of districts in academic achievement and growth. Beyond academic achievement and social and emotional development, the Ross School District has emerged as a beacon for innovation, creating more than 65 different electives, from virtual game design to broadcast journalism, and sponsoring the first TEDxYouth event in the Bay Area; the district is also in the process of creating a service-learning and community engagement program for all students to serve the local and global community.

Prior to serving as a superintendent, Dr. McDowell served as an associate superintendent of instructional and personnel services and as a high school principal of a Title I and California Distinguished School. Before entering administration, he was a leadership and instructional coach consulting with schools, districts, higher educational institutions, and state departments on educational leadership, teaching leadership, and instruction. Additionally, Dr. McDowell has several years of teaching experience in middle and high school science and mathematics.

Dr. McDowell serves as the chair of the advisory board for One Percent of Education, charged with facilitating leading experts in shaping a national narrative for advancing public education. Additionally, Dr. McDowell serves on the School of Environmental Leadership board tasked with supporting the organization in scaling innovation in secondary school environments. He is an international presenter, speaking on instruction, learning, leadership, and innovation. He is an author and consultant with Corwin Press, providing services in problem- and project-based learning, teaching and learning, systems and site leadership, and the Visible Learning Series. He is the author of *Rigorous PBL by Design: Three Key Shifts for Developing Confident and Competent Learners* (2017).

Previously, Dr. McDowell was a National Faculty member for the Buck Institute of Education and an advisor to educational organizations focused on equity, excellence, and innovation. His practical expertise in schools and systems is complemented by his scholarly approach to leadership, learning, and instruction. He holds a BS, an MA, and an EdD. Dr. McDowell and his wife, Quinn, live in Northern California with their two children, Harper and Asher.

Setting the Stage

When we study the biographies of our heroes, we learn that they spent years in preparation doing tiny, decent things before one historical moment propelled them to center stage. Moments, as if animate, use the prepared to tilt empires.

—Danusha Veronica Goska (2004)

Are We as Leaders Ready to Prepare All Learners for the 21st Century?

Over the past decade, I have had the opportunity and privilege to wrestle with this question as I served as classroom teacher, principal, associate superintendent, and superintendent. I have also had the wonderful opportunity to work with and advise schools around the world to improve student learning. I have had the opportunity to engage with some of the most innovative schools and the most traditional schools, each with mixed results in terms of motivation, academic development, and engagement. My work has focused on ensuring that education leaders implement practices that are best for all kids.

Throughout this pursuit, I have observed how difficult it is for leaders to balance stakeholders' demands that children on the one hand develop their reading, writing, and mathematical knowledge and skills and on the other hand their collaboration, critical thinking, and creativity skills.

Leaders have routinely asked me these two questions:

- How do we ensure that learners are prepared and competitive for the expectations of universities and colleges?
- How do we ensure that our learners are prepared for today and tomorrow's society and workforce?

The tension in this balancing act is evident when educators walk over to me with copies of "innovation" books under one arm—for example:

Creating Innovators: The Making of Young People Who Will Change the World (2012) by Tony Wagner

World Class Learners: Educating Creative and Entrepreneurial Students (2012) by Yong Zhao

Creative Confidence: Unleashing the Creative Potential Within Us All (2013) by Tom Kelley and David Kelley

Hip Hop Genius: Remixing High School Education (2011) by San Seidel

and books advocating for traditional strategies under the other arm—such as:

Visible Learning: Maximizing Impact on Learning for Teachers (2011) by John Hattie

Why Don't Students Like School? A Cognitive Scientist Answers Questions About How the Mind Works and What It Means for the Classroom (2009) by Daniel Willingham

Embedded Formative Assessment: Practical Strategies and tools for K–12 Teachers (2011) by Dylan Wiliam

They ask, "How do I integrate the innovative learning of tomorrow with the traditional strategies that we know build the key knowledge and skills needed for today?" The daunting challenge of ensuring students have core academic knowledge and skills that are required in the information age while simultaneously developing the 21st-century skills and experiencing 21st-century learning environments is an ever-present reality educational leaders face today.

Often communities make a choice on whether to focus on a more "traditional" path of learning, arguing that core academic knowledge and skills should be the focus of schooling where other communities deem 21st-century learning to be the sine qua non of the schooling experience.

As we will see, such a dichotomy limits our decision-making, instigating a devastating impact on learning and learners. Leaders must transcend such a false choice and rather focus on the substantial progress of 20th- and 21st-century learning for all children.

The Driving Question: Are Our Decisions Leading the Learning?

The question we need to ask ourselves is, *As leaders, how do we ensure that our decisions are substantially causing learning for all students in core academic knowledge and 21st-century skills?* Over the past few years, I have seen more and more binary leadership approaches often framing schools and systems as needing to take an "innovative" path or a "traditional" path to moving student learning forward. This binary thinking became most vividly apparent to me when I viewed *Most Likely to Succeed*, a film focused on students who left traditional schooling environments for High Tech High—a project-based charter designed to prepare children for the 21st century (Whiteley, 2015). High Tech High is esteemed by many educators and has been cited in numerous articles and books including Tony Wagner's bestseller *Creating Innovators* (2012). The argument made in the film is that student learning in the 21st century requires a fundamental redesign or reimagination of the educational model—no more desks, rows, silence, testing, and direct instruction from the all-knowing teacher. Instead, High Tech High offers students a high level of autonomy in their learning, a focus on curation and product development, and an expectation of collaboration and student-centered decision-making to solve rich, authentic tasks.

During the climax of the film, a mother is struggling with her decision to send her child to High Tech High because she worries that the academic foundations may be lacking. She is torn by a desire to ensure that her child receives an excellent foundation in academic skills while also desiring that her child benefit from the student choice, collaboration, and creativity that the school offers. As I watched her weigh the trade-offs of accepting the school's approach to innovative methods over traditional practices, I wondered how such extremes have come to pass in various schools around the country. Subsequent scenes of the film show students building stages, performing plays, and constructing apparatuses while collaborating with others. Teachers intentionally shied away from directive feed-back, instruction, or any recognizable educational intervention. It was evident that faculty strove not to engage in traditional reading, writing, and academic discourse and direct instruction and feedback. I left the theater wondering what would happen to the learners in High Tech High and as well as the learners in the traditional school depicted in the film. Moreover, I worried about the mother who struggled with having to make a choice between academic rigor and real-world relevance for her child. Are those really the options families must face for their children?

I believe that educators need not make a binary choice between traditional academic rigor and 21st-century skills. In this book I argue that school leaders must embrace both knowledge and skill sets and work to ensure that all of the students in their care receive the interventions necessary to progress toward traditional and innovative outcomes so that children will be prepared for tomorrow's workforce and society. The argument in this book is that leaders transcend from creating innovative or traditional academic schools or school systems and focus on creating *impactful* systems that focus on ensuring students and staff are getting more than one year's growth in one year's time in core academic content and 21st-century skills.

As we will see in future chapters, almost every action we take in a school works and the impact of such actions, particularly those that are instructional in nature, vary depending on students' competency (Hattie, 2009; Hattie & Donoghue, 2016). For instance, Hattie and Donoghue (2016) illustrate that the impact specific learning strategies have on student learning is related to the level of complexity students are working toward (Figure 1.1). For instance, exploring errors and misconceptions have a far greater effect on learning when students already possess surface-level knowledge than when they are first learning the material (Hattie & Donoghue, 2016).

The idea of orienting strategies to levels of learning is, of course, not new as Marzano (2007) illustrated strategies to be used when students are interacting with new knowledge (i.e., surface), practicing and deepening understanding of new knowledge (i.e., deep), and generating and testing hypotheses (transfer). Hattie and Donoghue (2016) point to certain strategies, such as problem- and project-based learning, that are impactful when students already possess a comprehensive understanding of knowledge and skills (e.g., surface and deep knowledge), whereas the methodology is less than ideal when students are initially learning material. Beyond learning and instructional strategies, feedback strategies follow the

Figure 1.1 Levels of Complexity

Levels of Complexity	Description
Surface	I can define/label idea(s) or use skill(s) (but I can't connect the ideas and skills together)
Deep	I can relate idea(s) or connect skill(s) (but I can't apply the ideas and skills in different situations)
Transfer	I can apply idea(s) or skill(s) in different situations

Conceptual understanding vs. Problem Solving

same logic; aligning to levels of complexity enhances student learning (Hattie & Timperley, 2007).

The argument here is that our pursuit should be on ensuring learners are gaining more than one year in their learning with an equal intensity of basic knowledge (surface knowledge) and that of deeper learning (deep and transfer learning). Without this understanding, leaders will orient staff toward specific methods or a grandiose vision of creating "21st-century schools" or "academic schools," rather than focusing on ensuring all students learn at high levels (i.e., surface, deep, and transfer) across a broad range of outcomes. Leaders will discard tried and true practices that have for centuries enabled students to learn how to multiply fractions, read an expository text, and write a poem in the pursuit of projects, virtual reality, and vodcasts (or the other way around). We must move away from the fixation of a school based on a philosophy of innovative or traditionalism and the mutual exclusivity of specific instructional methodologies over another and focus rather on how children learn and how children can take command of their learning across a broad range of outcomes and levels of complexity. We must lead by focusing on learning. Such a focus requires a few key leadership practices—tiny, decent things that are essential to learning for all. Leaders need to focus on how people learn and orient their decisions on ensuring people learn core academics and 21st-century learning deeply. As we will see, the focus of leaders and their corresponding actions have a dramatic impact on learning. We must think deeply about how students learn and from that understanding develop an approach to engaging with people as they learn, scaling our work, and making an impact on learning through our participation and promotion of learning. This requires a new type of educational leadership.

⤙ A New Leadership Focus

This book proposes leaders take on the role of a *lead learner*, focusing on cognitive (i.e., how people learn) and improvement science (i.e., how people get better at learning) and spending less time focusing on the traditional roles of educational leaders (see Figure 1.1). Unfortunately, contemporary educational leadership research shies away from the underpinning of student and staff learning and focuses squarely on creating the conditions for effective teacher practice (transformational leadership) or orienting leaders to focus on teachers' actions to participate in specific instructional practices (instructional leadership) (see Figure 1.2). Though the research has shown that instructional leaders have a far greater effect on student learning than transformational leadership, these two styles are not mutually exclusive in practice (Hattie, 2009; Robinson, 2011). For example, in order to engage in classroom observations, educational leaders must also be effective at buffering external demands, setting direction, and being accessible to staff.

In systems that integrate 20th- and 21st-century learning, both instructional and transformation leadership are necessary. Leaders must utilize a wide range of leadership strategies at their disposal to meet the learning demands of students and staff. As will be shown, the transformational demands of the 21st century are easily embraced and scaled whereas the attributes of the instructional leader of the 20th century are less popular but essential to student learning.

Figure 1.2   Instructional vs. Transformational Leadership Focus

Instructional Leadership	Transformational Leadership
• Classroom observations • Interpreting test scores with teachers • Focusing on instructional issues • Ensuring a coordinated instructional program • Highly visible • Communicating high academic standards • Ensuring class atmospheres are conducive to learning	• Inspirational motivation • Individualized support • Sets direction • Vision, group goals, high-performance expectations • Instructional support • Monitoring school activity • Buffering staff from external demands • Fair and equitable staffing • Easily accessible • High degree of autonomy for the school

Source: Hattie, 2009—based on Cognition's *Foundation Series.*

As such, the instructional and transformational dichotomies are not particularly helpful in clarifying the role of today's leader and the actions they should take in developing systems and supporting staff in preparing students to use core academic content and 21st-century skills (i.e., conative and cognitive skills; see Figure 1.3) in real-world contexts. These typologies don't require leaders to fundamentally orient nor anchor all of their decision-making to improving learning. Leaders should never have fidelity to a particular instructional strategy or program but rather should have integrity to the substantial learning of students and staff. The argument here is that leaders today need to base their role and decision-making on learning of staff and students and their current level of understanding on key outcomes (see Figure 1.3 as an example). Leaders must ensure more than

Figure 1.3   Criteria for Leader Decision-Making

What do students need to learn?	What does complexity look like in learning?	How do people learn?
The Three Cs: Content, Conative, Cognitive *Content*—understand core academic content at varying levels of complexity. *Conative skills (21st-century skills)*—have the skills for self-awareness and self-management and social awareness and social management. *Cognitive (21st-century skills)*—have the skills to analyze and use information to solve complex problems.	**Levels of Complexity: Surface, Deep, Transfer** *Surface* refers to a learner's ability to understand single or multiple ideas, but they are limited by the relationship of ideas and to a larger principle or skill set. *Deep* refers to a learner's ability to relate multiple ideas. This level describes the ability to understand similarities and differences between concepts and skills. *Transfer* refers to a learner's ability to apply simple and deep-level understanding and skills to a challenging problem within and between contexts.	**Learning Principles to Live By** Students and teachers recognize the importance of the following principles in their learning and that of their colleagues and peers: – Deliberate practice – Prior knowledge – Cognitive load – Social learning – (Re)-investing in learning

one year's growth in one year's time for students, staff, and, themselves on the outcomes listed in Figure 1.3. Figure 1.3 focuses leaders on ensuring that the decisions they are making are related to precisely what students need to learn, the progression students take when learning core content, and how students learn.

VOICES FROM THE FIELD

Gavin Hays, Lead Learner

Catholic Dioceses of Parramatta

Sydney, Australia

As a leader, it has been a difficult journey trying to progress both the core academic content and 21st-century skill agendas. For example, a few years ago as an assistant principal we focused our effort on ensuring our 14- to 15-year-old students improved their overall academic results on the Higher School Certificate exit examinations. A key component of this journey was the implementation of project-based learning across all key-learning areas in years 9 and 10. The vision was engagement, and we definitely achieved this objective; however, our results did not substantially increase. We had a strong focus on the development of 21st-century skills, including collaboration, communication, and critical thinking, so what was missing?

After we initiated this work we looked at the content that we were addressing in our projects, and we were horrified with some of the trade-offs we had made. We had reduced the opportunities that students had to read informative texts and write using different text types and replaced them with Google searching and iMovies. On the surface the students seemed engaged, but our projects lacked academic rigor and often did not create any sustained cognitive dissonance. However, we made another big mistake!

Like a pendulum that moves from side to side, we moved away from focusing on the student development of their 21st-century skill sets and focused just on core academic content. Again, there was no substantial improvement in academic results. Going back to our focus on substantial learning in both core content and 21st-century skills, we narrowed the focus and found we were able to engage students and develop their skills, providing them with quality content and rigorous tasks, and provide exceptional teaching and feedback at all levels of learning; as a result, we saw increases in academic achievement.

Within three years the school was consistently in the 100 top-performing high schools and was recognized internationally as a center of innovation and academic excellence utilizing project- and problem-based learning and the flipped classroom to develop both the 21st-century skills and core academic content of students. This experience helped me as a leader understand the relationship between content and skills, and the need to ensure that support is given to both students and teachers in developing both simultaneously.

A *lead learner* is needed in today's educational environment. A lead learner is someone whose core purpose is substantially enhancing the learning of students and staff. Lead learners focus on improvement by centering their decisions on the progress and proficiency of student and staff learning. They model effective learning in their daily practices and short- and long-term decisions. Anchoring decision-making to learning, in many ways, requires leaders take an *ambidextrous approach* to how they design and organize schools and systems of schools. By ambidextrous approach, this text refers to a leader who focuses on the learning of all students and staff by standardizing aspects of the educational system that ensure specific learning-centered criteria are developed, replicated, and scaled across the school system. Simultaneously, ambidextrous refers to a leader who focuses on customizing strategies or pathways that ensure students and staff have the flexibility to deploy and augment strategies that substantially impact learning in the classroom. *Merriam-Webster* defines ambidextrous (as "able to use both hands equally well; unusually skillful" ("ambidextrous," 2017). In this book, we substitute the term *hands* with the concept of the left and right brain. The left brain is often referred to as the standardized, logical, sequential, convergent aspects of the brain while the right side of the brain is customizable, creative, divergent, emotional, and relational. The split-brain theory (i.e., right brain–left brain) theory is a Nobel Prize–winning theory by Roger W. Sperry (1968). Though this has been contested for decades, conceptually and colloquially people associate intuitive, creative thinking to the right hemisphere of the brain and analytical thinking to the left hemisphere. This metaphor is used here to illustrate the standardized and customizable approaches leaders must take to meet the learning needs of staff and students in exponentially complex times and complex organizations.

Figure 1.4 illustrates the key differences between "left" and "right" brain educational leaders based on the typical typology of the actions associated with each hemisphere. It is important to note that Figure 1.4 emphasizes student learning as the main focus of left- and right-brain leaders.

Figure 1.4   Left- and Right-Brain Leaders

	Left-Brain Leaders	Right-Brain Leaders
Why?	To develop educational systems that ensure students are prepared for college	To develop educational systems that prepare students for the 21st-century economy
How?	Design efficient processes and establish structures that produce the highest percentage of students to gain entry into university	Design a variety of processes and structures that maximize student experiences for being prepared for their future outside of school
What?	Tight coherence of systems Direct staff actions to maximize efficiency	Loose coherence of systems High level of voice and choice for staff

Ensuring Clarity, Coherence, and Capacity: Crafting Improved Leadership Skills

This book was written to orient leader thinking and behavior to the learning of children and staff—that is, to focus their actions and beliefs on what creates a substantial impact on student and adult learning across a system. The administrator who dives into the lead learner approach will see the need to design an educational system that integrates left- and right-brain approaches by doing the following:

1. Ensure *clarity* in strategic planning to illuminate the goals and boundaries of the organization's work and articulate the flexibility in approaching student and staff learning. For example, leaders strike a balance between the tensions of surface and deep learning by creating a focused strategic plan that articulates the equity (i.e., every child will show substantial growth in learning) and the excellence demands (i.e., meeting content and 21st-century competencies) of all learners. This requires an integrity to specific learning principles while embracing autonomy toward potential solutions in schools and classrooms.

2. Establish *coherence* in learning expectations for students' achievement and progress throughout the educational system and in determining the right people for ensuring such student performance while ensuring the highest levels of flexibility in how practitioners teach and intervene.

3. Enact organizational *capacity*-building processes that ensure teachers are constantly learning independently and collaboratively through their monitoring of practice as it relates to the learning of children. Such practices are shared across the system and used to organize further professional learning and develop models of best practice across the organization.

4. *Crafting* their own personal leaderships skills to move learning forward for all stakeholders.

CONCLUSION

Today's demands for learners to be prepared for college and career are vastly different from the past. All children must be college and career ready—not just a few. Moreover, all children must be equipped with the knowledge and skills necessary to navigate in the 21st century and that such outcomes are learned deeply (i.e., surface, deep, and transfer). The social and emotional, creative problem-solving, and academic reading, writing, and speaking outcomes required of students require teachers to be flexible and directive in their instructional approach. Educational leaders must model such adaptive and directive approaches in their daily life and through the systems they develop and maintain. From the systems level, leaders must establish clarity through planning, coherence in what is defined and what is autonomous between and among departments, institute ongoing capacity building, and craft personal leadership skills to embrace and handle scaling the work of impact across a system.

This book walks leaders through the steps necessary to build systems and refine skills that will meet the learning demands for all staff and students. Chapters 2–5 focus on the key elements of the lead learner (i.e., clarity, coherence, and capacity). Specifically, these chapters provide actions leaders can take to create an organization that continuously makes the impact we desire for student 20th- and 21st-century learning. Chapter 6 lays out a set of actions leaders can take to ensure their personal leadership models and enables others to make the right decisions for learning for all. With practical examples, stories from the field, and numerous activities and reflective questions, this book walks leaders through the steps necessary to engage in the work of the lead learner. This book will enable you to move from choosing between a *rigorous* school system and an *innovative* school system to an *impactful* school system.

REFLECTION QUESTIONS

1. What do you know now that you didn't know when you started reading?

2. What questions are you facing as a leader? Do the questions posed in Chapter 1 resonate with the tensions you are facing as a leader?

3. In your mind, what is the key difference between being an instructional leader and a lead learner?

4. How would you support someone in explaining the need to transition from an instructional leader to a lead learner?

5. Based on your experience, which aspect of the lead learner—clarity, coherence, and capacity—resonates with you?

6. Based on your experience, what aspects of the "ambidextrous approach" resonates with your approach to leadership? What aspects appear challenging to your leadership decisions?

7. When you walk away from this book, what do you expect the key outcomes to be?

ACTIVITIES

The following activities focus leaders on identifying their leadership tendencies toward "right" brain and "left" brain approaches in given leadership situations.

ACTIVITY 1.1: AMBIDEXTROUS APPROACH TO LEADERSHIP PROFILE ASSESSMENT

Step 1: Self-Assessment: Measuring Personal Leadership Dexterity

Figure 1.5   Measuring Personal Leadership Dexterity

Measuring Personal Leadership Dexterity				
I'm a firm believer that inquiry-based methods of instruction are the most important pedagogical approaches to learning.				
Strongly Disagree	Disagree	Neutral	Agree	Strongly Agree
I believe that providing my staff with autonomy regarding teaching and learning is the most appropriate professional decision for ensuring students learn at high levels.				
Strongly Disagree	Disagree	Neutral	Agree	Strongly Agree
I believe that professional development is for input of new content information and not primarily used for collective problem-solving with staff.				
Strongly Disagree	Disagree	Neutral	Agree	Strongly Agree
I'm very involved in looking at evidence of student performance data with teachers and making decisions in light of the staff discussions.				
Strongly Disagree	Disagree	Neutral	Agree	Strongly Agree
I'm actively involved in all professional development that impacts student learning.				
Strongly Disagree	Disagree	Neutral	Agree	Strongly Agree
Students need to know their basic reading, writing, and arithmetic.				
Strongly Disagree	Disagree	Neutral	Agree	Strongly Agree
There are multiple ways to make a decision.				
Strongly Disagree	Disagree	Neutral	Agree	Strongly Agree
At the end of the day, students need to know core academic content and 21st-century skills.				
Strongly Disagree	Disagree	Neutral	Agree	Strongly Agree
Pacing guides, strictly aligned curriculum, and assessment are paramount for our success.				
Strongly Disagree	Disagree	Neutral	Agree	Strongly Agree
The majority of our staff meetings are focused on learning and teaching.				
Strongly Disagree	Disagree	Neutral	Agree	Strongly Agree

Step 2: Determining Leadership Tendencies

Once you complete the assessment, take a look at your responses. If you selected "Agree" or "Strongly Agree" on questions 1 and 2, then you have a tendency toward right-brain approaches. If you selected "Agree" or "Strongly Agree" on questions 3, 6, and 9, you have a tendency toward left-brain approaches. If you selected "Agree" or "Disagree" on questions 4, 5, 7, 8, and 10, then you are more aligned to ambidextrous leadership responses. After reviewing your responses, complete the next activity.

ACTIVITY 1.2: IDENTIFYING PERSONAL LEADERSHIP NEXT STEPS

The following activity allows leaders to assess their focus on learning, their skill set in moving learning forward, and identifying the system readiness of their organization to substantially enhance student learning. Moreover, the following activity provides an opportunity for leaders to reflect on key questions, needs, and potential next steps in their work.

Figure 1.6 Rating Current Leadership Capacity Across Key Success Criteria

The Lead Learner Success Criteria

Learning Intention: To ensure *all* learners and faculty develop, substantially progress toward, and apply a proportional level of content, cognitive, and conative knowledge and skills (surface, deep, and transfer) in their work.

Elements of the Lead Learner	Success Criteria	Rating
Clarity Develops and executes a lean strategic planning process	• Strategic plan focuses the district on growth and criterion goals related to equity, engagement, and excellence. • Leadership team has used tools to assess system progress toward and proficiency of equity, engagement, and excellence outcome before making plans of action. • Leadership has devised a strategic plan that articulates competing theories of action, the learning needs of the organization, a narrative to cascade across the organization, and routines for inspecting performance.	+1 0 −1
Coherence Aligns all systems to ensure substantial impact on 21st-century skills and content goals	• Consistent growth and proficiency expectations for students are established and are consistent regardless of school, classroom, or teacher. • Standardized learning intentions and success criteria across schools and classroom are established.	+1 0 −1

Elements of the Lead Learner	Success Criteria	Rating
	• Standardized criteria for surface, deep, and transfer levels are established in the system. • Customizable approaches to teaching at varying levels of complexity (i.e., surface, deep, and transfer) are articulated in the organization. • Personnel systems ensure expectations of staff are clearly articulated, candidates are filtered, structured interviews are deployed, interviews and demonstrations are required, and targeted feedback and support is ongoing and consistent.	
Capacity Builds system-wide capacity	• Leaders center professional learning on student progress and proficiency (more than 90% of their time). • Leaders ensure professional learning is job embedded and involves inspection of impact on students. • Leaders ensure that learning is shared across the system. • Leaders select from a variety of organizational routines, including critical friends teams, student involvement in the CFT process, learning rounds, learning convenings (meeting reboots), and professional learning events.	+1 0 −1
Crafting Builds personal leadership skills to lead the learning	• Establishes norms that promote and ensure staff are learning and are engaging in decision-making that is linked to student learning. • Uses structured processes for exploring ideas and narrowing in on decisions that cause learning. • Practices strategies that are expected of educators in their work.	+1 0 −1

+1 = Criteria are routinely achieved.

0 = Criteria are being discussed but routine implementation is nonexistent.

−1 = Elements are not part of the organization or the leader's actions.

ACTIVITY 1.3: NEEDS ASSESSMENT

Review the bullets under "Scope," "Systems," and "Skills." In the first area, under "Scope," identify whether you think your school or system has a key focus on developing students' 21st-century skills, focuses on core academic competency, ensures a proportional level of understanding (i.e., surface, deep, and transfer), focuses on growth and proficiency, and ensures all students have an opportunity and support system in place to meet these demands. Reflect on the following questions:

- How do you make such a determination? What systems are in place (or absent) that brought you to such a conclusion? What policies or procedures assisted you in your decision? What role have you played in this determination?

Next, consider your system readiness regarding the scope of your school or educational system. Identify whether you think the system/school is clear on expectations and has processes in place to continually focus on said expectations. Second, identify whether you believe there is coherence across organizational functions (i.e., human resources, finance, governance, educational services).
Reflect on the following questions:

- How you make such a determination? What systems are in place (or absent) that brought you to such a conclusion? What policies or procedures assisted you in your decision? What role have you played in this determination?

Finally, consider your skill set regarding the scope of your school or educational system and the systems that are currently in place. Identify your strengths and weaknesses regarding developing the organization, facilitating stakeholders in decision-making, and ensuring that plans are put into place that focus on learning.

Figure 1.7   System-Wide Needs Assessment

Scope *The key areas of focus for schools and educational systems*	**Systems** *The specific structures and processes that enable schools and educational systems to meet educational outcomes*	**Skills** *Specific leadership skills that are necessary to enable leaders to be successful in meeting the educational outcomes of all children*
- 21st-century skills (conative and cognitive knowledge and skills) - Core academic competency - Proportional level of surface, deep, and transfer learning - Growth and proficiency - Equity (all students)	- Clarity - Coherence - Capacity	- Agreements - Protocols - Modeling

ACTIVITY 1.4: WHAT ARE KEY QUESTIONS THAT YOU HAVE AS YOU MOVE FORWARD IN YOUR LEADERSHIP?

Figure 1.8   Guideposts

The following strategies are aimed at providing proximity to practice and as such offer concrete approaches within the areas of the four Cs.

Guideposts	Description	Strategy	Questions That Emerge
Stay small, stay focused	Almost everything in education works. Limit initiatives to what makes a substantial impact on learning.	• Focus on growth of 20th- and 21st-century outcomes for all • Substantially limit initiatives • Clarify what you are *not* going to do	
Take an Ambidextrous Approach	We often think in "either/or" rather than "both/and" terms, limiting our ability to make innovative and impactful decisions.	• Articulate standardized and customizable features in your organization • Provide support for students to learn and teachers to teach at surface, deep, and transfer levels	
Avoid Solution Fixation	We tend to focus on solutions rather than the criteria for success. We need to reverse this trend.	• Center instructional and personnel decisions on success criteria rather than solutions	

Guideposts	Description	Strategy	Next Steps
Anchor on impact	Our impact on learning is mostly hidden from us and as such we need to unmask the evidence of our impact on learning to make key decisions that directly impact the learning of others.	• Ensure that beliefs and actions are understood before making personnel decisions • Establish processes to inspect impact on learning • Align capacity-building activities to those influences that make the greatest impact on student learning	
Model Learning	Certain leadership strategies have a higher probability of enhancing learning of students. Leaders need to model strategies that make the greatest impact.	• Model what you expect in the classroom • Utilize agreements and protocols that promote focus and flexibility • Establish different meeting types to enable focus and flexibility	

NEXT STEPS

1. Write down three key personal leadership goals that you want to focus on to ensure a lead learner approach. As you engage in this process, consider the following reflective questions: *How do these goals relate to one another? Where are my strengths? Where would my leadership team lean?*

2. Identify key questions that you have going into the areas of clarity, coherence, and capacity. Write down what you think you already know in these areas. At the end of each chapter go back and see if there are differences in what you know and what is being presented.

3. Identify a way in which you would present this information to your executive team, school board, staff, community, and parents.

2

Clarity

Strategic Planning

I have always found that plans are useless, but planning is indispensable.

—Dwight D. Eisenhower (1957)

A few years ago, a veteran superintendent stated to me that the most important part of being an educational leader and teacher is being explicit about what I'm *not* going to spend my team's and organization's time, energy, and effort on. With a smile, he went further and said, "You should follow the sage advice of Anna in the movie *Frozen* and 'let it go.'" Throughout my career in multiple roles within and between schools and school systems, I have learned the sheer power and immeasurable difficulty of following such sage advice. In fact, the idea of "staying small and staying focused" on a few initiatives in my mind requires bold and courageous leadership in articulating what a class, department, school, or system *is* and *is not* going to do. Frankly, in my experience, everything in education is designed to pull me and my organization away from the learning of children and staff.

The key is to stay small and stay focused on what will make a substantial impact on students and staff. This is easier said than done! *Why?* Because almost everything in education works! Granted, not everything has the same impact on learning but everything that is in education has an advocate, and when educators come together with other stakeholders to develop a purpose and plan for the school they craft a document that is inclusive of everything and accountable to nothing. If you don't believe me, take a look at most strategic plans and one can easily make sense of the massive compendium of initiatives and priorities of a district. As Reeves and Flach (2011) have shown, there is an inverse relationship between the size of a strategic plan and the impact of the district on student learning. If such a point needs to be highlighted in the literature, school districts are clearly overloaded with initiatives, plans, and inspections (Reeves & Flach, 2011).

Narrowing down the number of initiatives to ensure clarity is no easy feat, as the initiatives that have a substantial impact on student learning are often far less popular to implement because of two primary reasons:

1. **Structural changes are more popular than behavioral change:** Influences that have the greatest impact on student learning require behavioral change (such as refining our feedback practices or building stronger teacher and student relationships) as opposed to structural changes (e.g., changing the school calendar or changing the schedule).

2. **Past experience:** Those changes that make a substantial impact on learning are often not focused on in preservice teaching or consistently developed over time in schools. On top of that, most teachers did not consistently experience such practices when they were students and they often perceived their school experience as beneficial and want to replicate their experience for others.

The suggestion in this chapter is for leaders to establish a planning process that goes directly toward ensuring growth for all learners and articulating where the school system will and will not focus its resources. The plan is an artifact of the current iteration of thinking and doing—a line etched in sand—and is the byproduct of the much more important process of leading others to think deeply about learning and how a system causes learning for all. This is done by having stakeholders engage in three questions.

Three Questions That Ensure Clarity in Strategic Planning

To focus the organization on substantially enhancing learning for all, lead learners must center their work on three fundamental questions that have been found to be essential to ensuring learning is visible for learners (Hattie, 2009). These questions include, *Where are we going?*, *Where are we now?*, and *What's next?* These questions serve as the means to clarify the purpose, outcomes or "end in mind" for the organization (i.e., where are we going?), a clear understanding of current performance or status (i.e., where are we now?), and to identify next steps (i.e., what's next?) to alleviate the discrepancy between current performance and their expectations.

Question 1: Where Are We Going?

Click on your school's or district's website and write down the number of times you clicked your mouse to find a page that had the word "learner," "student," "progress," and "proficiency" integrated in some way. Chances are the sporting news, the financials, and the leisure sections filled the information on your website before such headlines emerged.

Beyond the issue of burying the lead, if your overall purpose is longer than a tweet and is not focused on the progress, proficiency, and cognitive and emotional engagement of children, you need to make a change. This is about clarifying exactly your outcome so that you can anchor all organizational decisions and clarify your intentions to everyone. Take a look at Stonefields School's core purpose: to cause learning and to serve each learner. It's clear, concise, and serves as a filter for what you are about. Plus, this is on page one with several videos to depict what that message means. (More on story building in a later section.)

> *The key to question 1 is to ensure clarity and focus related to the school system's purpose.*

This text recommends creating a simple message that paints the expected outcome for your organization, such as to cause learning and to serve each learner. Such a statement should encapsulate the three Es:

- Equity imperative (all children)
- Engagement (emotional and cognitive focus)
- Excellence (high levels of learning in core content and 21st-century skills)

If your purpose does not encapsulate the three Es, then you should go back to the questions in the introduction and reflect on what tension is pulling you away from (a) all children, (b) engaging kids, and (c) ensuring students are learning at high levels. If your purpose goes beyond the three Es, then you should reflect on how much emphasis is being taken away from what matters most.

Question 2: Where Are We Now?

Having answered question 1, we have established the core purpose of learning. Now, we need to understand the current state of affairs in relationship to student learning performance in content and 21st-century knowledge and skills. Stated differently, we need to find evidence of where learners are in their learning.

The key to question 2 is to know your system's or school's impact on student learning.

This requires leaders to use a series of tools (see Figure 2.1 below for a sample; several others are included in the Appendix) to capture evidence of student learning. Once data are collected, leaders need to synthesize the data, identifying key facts and patterns that emerge, and then develop inferences that they draw from the data (see Figure 2.2).

Figure 2.1   Sample Tool for Capturing Data

🙂 Learner Survey: Kindergarten – Second Grade			
1. My teacher often checks whether I'm understanding the work.	YES	NO	😐
2. My teacher helps me achieve things I didn't think that I could.	YES	NO	😐
3. My teacher thinks that everyone can learn.	YES	NO	😐
4. My teacher helps me with my learning.	YES	NO	😐
5. My teacher understands where I'm at with my learning.	YES	NO	😐
6. My teacher helps me at the right level for me in a way that I understand.	YES	NO	😐

	Learner Survey: Kindergarten – Second Grade			
7. My teacher has conversations with me.		YES	NO	☹
8. My teacher pushes me to try things that are hard.		YES	NO	☹
9. My teacher gives me time to figure things out.		YES	NO	☹
10. My teacher gives me feedback about my work.		YES	NO	☹
11. I trust my teacher.		YES	NO	☹
12. It is OK to make mistakes in my classroom.		YES	NO	☹
13. My teacher helps me understand how to learn.		YES	NO	☹

Figure 2.2 Data Synthesis

What do we notice? (FACTS ONLY—NO INFERENCES)	**What inferences do we draw?** (What is the story I'm telling about the data? What other stories could be told from the data?)
(For example) • Eighty percent of students stated they trusted the teacher, 15% said they didn't know, and 5% said they did not trust the teacher. • Sixty percent of students stated that they didn't think everyone can learn, 30% said they didn't know, and 10% said they believed all students can learn.	(For example) • The classroom is a safe place for children to learn and grow, and there are mixed signals of whether all children can learn and grow in the classroom. • We wonder what students (in terms of their performance) have this perception.

Question 3: What's Next?

The key to question 3 is to prepare for continuous improvement around your purpose.

The third question is related to continuous improvement and requires leaders to do a few things including,

- develop competing theories of action,
- determine the learning needs of the organization,
- develop a powerful story, and
- establish a routine of continual inspection.

Develop Competing Theories of Action

To begin, leaders review the inferences they drew from the past exercise and identify actions they would take to yield a high impact on the progress and proficiency of student learning. Leaders should push others to advocate for proposed actions with a rationale that includes research and past practices in the school (that are tied to data). Once the team has established a set of actions, they should write down all of the actions they are *not* going to engage in. One way to do this is to create a *theory of action*.

A theory of action is simply an "if/then" statement that concludes with an "as such" statement (see Figure 2.3). The first part of building the statement is to articulate the focus of the actions the organization is going to take (i.e., "if"), the second part of the statement

---

Figure 2.3   Sample Theory of Action

If we focus our priorities on developing students' surface-level knowledge within deeper learning contexts . . .

Then all learners will surpass one year's growth and have the knowledge and skills on basic-level competency assessments . . .

As such, the school/district will be focusing on

- ensuring clear learning intentions and success criteria that are differentiated between surface-, deep-, and transfer-level learning, and
- engaging in professional development that focuses on high-impact strategies that target surface learning.

(i.e., "then") articulates the outcome, and the "as such" articulates the detailed steps the organization will take.

Next, leaders need to articulate what they will not be focused on or what will not be happening any more or does not have the potential to be supported (see Figure 2.4).

Figure 2.4 Competing Theories of Action

Theory of Action	A	B
If . . .	If we focus our priority on developing students' surface-level knowledge within deeper learning contexts,	If we focus our priorities on broader structural interventions and deeper learning methodologies,
Then . . .	then all learners will surpass one year's growth and have the knowledge and skills on basic-level competency assessments.	then all learners will surpass one year's growth and have the knowledge and skills to be successful on basic-level competency assessments.
As such . . .	As such, the school/district will be investing in the following: Ensuring clear learning intentions and success criteria are differentiated between surface-, deep-, and transfer-level learning Engaging in professional development that focuses on high-impact strategies that target surface-level learning.	As such, the school/district will be investing in the following: Reducing class size Changing scheduling Investing additional resources on inquiry-based methodology.

Suggested ways of reviewing, critiquing, and generating the "if/then/as such" statements is using structured protocols. Figure 2.5 illustrates three protocols that may be used to generate priorities.

Figure 2.5 Protocols A, B, and C Related to Priorities

Protocol A: What?, So What?, Now What?

The following protocol allows participants to separate observations and facts from inferences/assumptions in order to make effective individual and collective decisions.

Suggested Time: 45 minutes

Opening Moves (Introduction) (5 minutes)

- Review purpose of protocol.
- Review agreements (or norms) of the team.
- Identify facilitator/participant and participants.

Statements of Problem/Challenge/Circumstance (10 minutes)

- The facilitator asks a participant to outline a current challenge/problem/or circumstance.
- The facilitator asks for clarifying questions from other participants.
- The facilitator then asks everyone to identify the facts of the challenge/ problem/circumstance. (What facts emerge from this challenge?)
- The facilitator populates that information onto a chart under the term "What?"

Mastering Our Stories—*So What?* (10 minutes)

- The facilitator then asks what appear to be inferences/assumptions that are drawn from the challenge (What are we assuming or taking for granted? What other assumptions may there be?). The facilitator populates this information onto a chart under the term "So What?"
- The facilitator asks the participants to consider all of the people who are impacted by this challenge and identify what assumptions they may possess in this challenge.

Taking Action—*Now What?* (10 minutes)

- Next, the facilitator asks each participant to write down three or four specific next steps on sticky notes. The facilitator provides the following prompts: What additional information do we need? What appear to be logical next steps in moving toward a solution?
- The facilitator asks the participants to silently place their sticky notes under a column titled "Next Steps." Participants may group the sticky notes quietly.
- The facilitator then asks the group to describe the groupings. (What appear to be the major themes related to next steps?)
- The facilitator asks the original participant if he or she would like to share next steps he or she is considering.
- The facilitator then asks the original participant when he or she should check back on action steps and outcomes.
- The session is then closed.

Protocol B: Critical Friends

The following protocol is designed for providing students and educators with specific feedback regarding a product, presentation, or process.

Suggested Time: 45 minutes

Opening Moves (Introduction) (5 minutes)

- Review purpose of protocol.
- Review agreements (or norms) of the team.
- Identify facilitator/participant and participants.
- Review success criteria of product, process, or presentation being evaluated.

Opening Presentation (5 minutes)

- The teacher, student, or leader requesting feedback provides a 10-minute overview on the product, process, or presentation.
- The facilitator will then ask the CFT for any clarifying questions.
- The presenter will provide answers to any clarifying questions.
- *This process can be much more effective when materials are provided before the CFT review. One suggestion is to e-mail all CFT members materials to be reviewed 72 hours before the CFT process.*

Strengths (I like) (10 minutes)

- Facilitator asks the CFT to provide feedback related to the strengths of the product, process, or presentation.
- CFT members will begin each piece of feedback using the following stems: "I like ___ because ____" or "One strength is ___ because ____." (Rationale should be related to success criteria.)
- *During the next three sections (Strengths, Questions, and Next Steps), the person receiving feedback should not make any remarks and should only listen and write down notes.*
- *The facilitator should ensure that all information is posted on the website.*

Questions (I wonder)

- Facilitator asks the CFT to provide questions for the presenter to think through the product, process, or presentation.
- CFT members will begin each piece of feedback using the following stems: "I wonder ____ because ____." or "One question to consider includes ___." (Rationale should be related to success criteria.)

Next Steps

- Facilitator asks the CFT to provide feedback related to the strengths of the product, process, or presentation.
- CFT members will begin each piece of feedback using the following stems: "One next step may be ____." "One idea to consider is _____." (Rationale should be related to success criteria.)

(Continued)

Figure 2.5 (Continued)

Closing Remarks

- The teacher receiving feedback has the opportunity to thank the CFT for their feedback and to provide specific next steps they will take in light of the feedback they received.

Protocol C: Let It Go

Purpose

The following protocol provides teams with a process for determining critical initiatives and eliminating or deprioritizing other initiatives.

Suggested Time: 45 minutes

Opening Moves (Introduction) (5 minutes)

- Review purpose of protocol.
- Review agreements (or norms) of the team.
- Identify facilitator/presenter and reviewers.

Procedure

- The team writes down every single initiative they are responsible for on separate sticky notes.
- The team then posts the notes on the wall in no particular order.
- The team is then tasked with categorizing the sticky notes on to the template below.
- *Columns:* One side is titled "Politics of Distraction" and the other is titled "Collaborative Expertise." The facilitator may define the "Politics of Distraction" as those initiatives that promote less than one year's growth in student learning. The facilitator may define "Collaborative Expertise" as those initiatives that promote more than one year's growth in one year's time.
- *Rows:* One row is titled "Within Our Control" and the other is titled "Not Within Our Control."
- Next the team answers the following questions:
  - What initiatives in quadrant 3 are we willing to "let go" of for our students?
  - What initiatives in quadrant 1 are we willing to bring forward to others as impending our team's ability to be successful?
  - What initiatives in quadrant 2 are we willing to continue to focus on and leverage?
  - What initiatives in quadrant 4 are we willing to bring forward to others as supporting our team's ability to be successful?
- The team determines next steps in light of these questions.

	Politics of Distraction (Less than .40 ES per year)	Collaborative Expertise (Less than .40 ES per year)
Within Our Control (of the District or School or Team)	1	2
Not Within Our Control (of the District or School or Team)	3	4

Closing Moves (5 minutes)

Ask participants to rate how well the team executed the protocol and followed agreements.

Source: McDowell, M. P. (2017). *Rigorous PBL by design.* Thousand Oaks, CA: Corwin.

Figure 2.6   SWOT Analysis

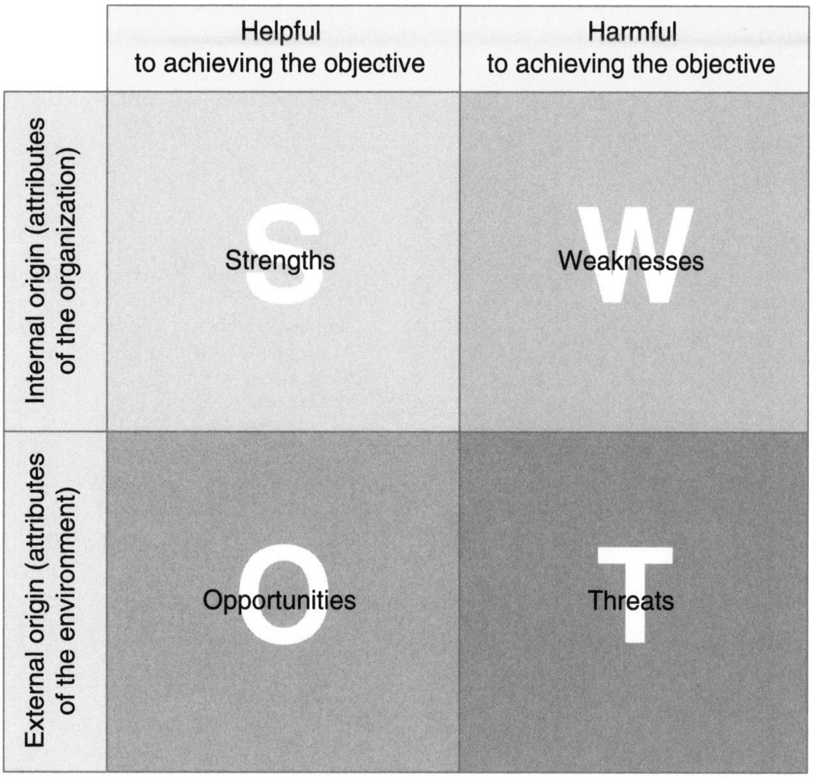

Source: Xhienne. CC BY-SA 2.5. https://creativecommons.org/licenses/by-sa/2.5/deed.en. SWOT Analyis Diagram in English Language. https://commons.wikimedia.org/wiki/File:SWOT_en.svg

Determine the Learning Needs of the Organization

Once a theory of action has been created, leaders need to conduct a needs assessment on what knowledge and skills their employees need to ensure that key outcomes are met. For example, in Figure 2.3, leaders need to identify the needs of the staff in the two key areas:

- *Ensuring clear learning intentions and success criteria are differentiated between surface, deep, and transfer levels*
- *Engaging in professional development that focuses on high-impact strategies that target surface learning*

Figure 2.6 (on the previous page) and Figure 2.7 (below) illustrate tools that support leaders in determining professional development needs. (Detailed facilitation notes are provided at the end of the chapter.) Figure 2.6, the SWOT Analysis, is used for leaders to

Figure 2.7 Sample SWOT Analysis

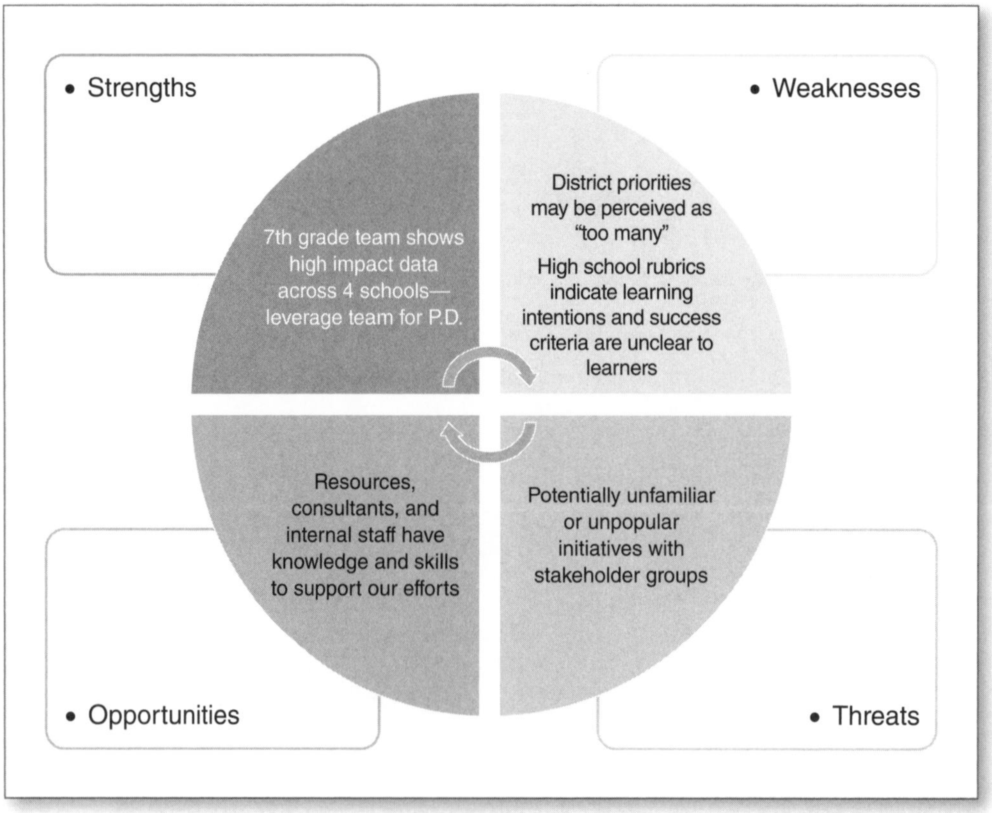

- Strengths

- Weaknesses

7th grade team shows high impact data across 4 schools—leverage team for P.D.

District priorities may be perceived as "too many"

High school rubrics indicate learning intentions and success criteria are unclear to learners

Resources, consultants, and internal staff have knowledge and skills to support our efforts

Potentially unfamiliar or unpopular initiatives with stakeholder groups

- Opportunities

- Threats

determine strengths (internal to the organization and helpful to achieve the priority), weaknesses (internal to the organization and harmful to achieve the priority), opportunities (external to the organization and helpful to achieve the priority), and threats (external to the organization and harmful to organization) for the organization related to building capacity for professional staff. Figure 2.8 illustrates a tool called a discrepancy analysis that allows leaders to define their desired state and their current reality and craft next steps to meet their goals (i.e., desired state). Figures 2.7 and 2.8 provide examples of the SWOT and discrepancy analysis, respectively.

Figure 2.8 Discrepancy Analysis

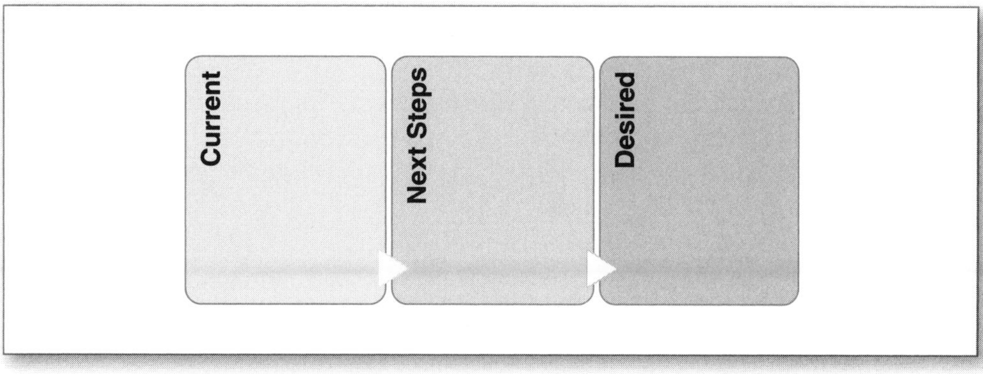

Current → **Next Steps** → **Desired**

Figure 2.9 Discrepancy Analysis Example

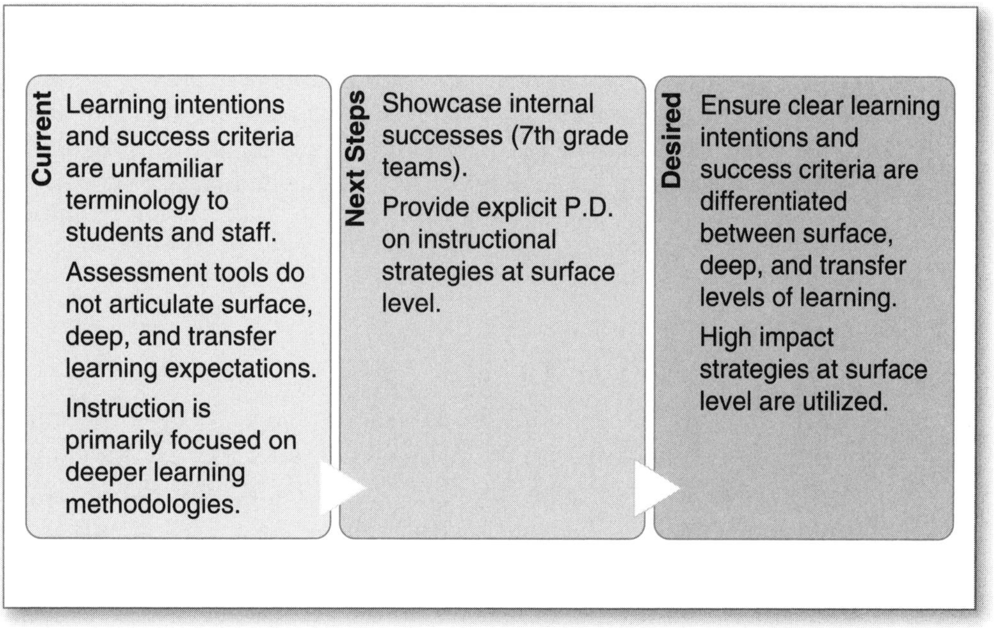

Current
Learning intentions and success criteria are unfamiliar terminology to students and staff.

Assessment tools do not articulate surface, deep, and transfer learning expectations.

Instruction is primarily focused on deeper learning methodologies.

Next Steps
Showcase internal successes (7th grade teams).

Provide explicit P.D. on instructional strategies at surface level.

Desired
Ensure clear learning intentions and success criteria are differentiated between surface, deep, and transfer levels of learning.

High impact strategies at surface level are utilized.

VOICES FROM THE FIELD

LaTyia Rolle, Principal

David Reese Elementary School

Sacramento, California

Having served as an elementary school principal at urban Title I schools, I've learned quite a bit in a short amount of time. Leadership takes tenacity, clarity, and most importantly confidence, to carry out the work! The challenges of Title I schools surpass those of non–Title I in unique ways. While there is always a level of character that comes into practice when you're charged with nurturing young minds, students in poverty experience education and school differently. The capacity to learn is great, but it should be executed quickly. Therefore, every lesson, strategy, and standards-based assessment must be directly connected to relevant content and given a clearly defined purpose upfront. One of the known and overly discussed challenges with our educational system today is the fact that there are far too many initiatives on the plates of teachers and site leaders. It's true; everyone is quick to jump into a debate about what should be added to the plate! Instead of that, my approach and those of my mentors has been removing any items on the plate that don't allow students to access subject matter in a meaningful way that in turn will allow for academic or social/emotional growth benefiting that learner. Students must see themselves as contributors to the learning environment and see their teachers as competent, compassionate adults that take learning seriously and cultivate a classroom culture that accepts progress and not perfection! As a leader, it's my role to serve. Serving students, their families, and the community is a huge piece of that. Serving my staff involves looking at our school culture. I'm making sure that I'm encouraging teachers to take the time to analyze their focus standards, assessment data, and lesson design consistently while strategically attaching meaning to every minute of instruction.

Develop a Powerful Story

One of the great levers educational leaders have is how they frame problems and challenges to their stakeholders. Left-brain leaders like to frame problems from an improvement or shortfall scenario. There is a danger in taking a deficit approach in an organization as it often leads to doubling down on past practice, blaming others, and narrowing practices to ensure basic skills are developed at all costs. On the other side of the equation, right-brain leaders love framing problems as "new ventures," casting away the "nothing new under the sun" adage and arguing for new outcomes (e.g., how do we prepare kids for globalization?), new initiatives (e.g., coding for all), and re-allocation of resources (e.g., teaching all kids to code).

This text recommends that leaders find a middle ground by framing as many challenges or problems as opportunities. The opportunity is that you have success stories in your building and system, the research and professional development experts are in arm's reach, and that the aim of growth for all learners is palatable and engaging for (most) stakeholders. Therefore, focus on selling a clear vision and mission to everyone with a sticky, pithy message.

To tell the story to others, we suggest using the script approach (see Figure 2.10) so eloquently presented by Daniel Pink (2013) in *To Sell Is Human: The Surprising Truth About Moving Others*, in which he describes how Pixar frames "the quick pitch" to form a connected message around a new movie project.

Figure 2.10   Script

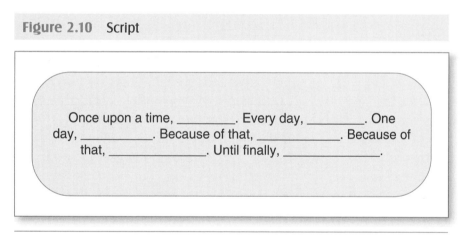

Source: Script developed by Dan Pink.

Here is an example from *Finding Nemo*.

Once upon a time, there was a widowed fish named Marlin who was extremely protective of his only son, Nemo. Every day, Marlin warned Nemo of the ocean's dangers and implored him not to swim far away. One day, in an act of defiance, Nemo ignores his father's warnings and swims into the open water. Because of that, he is captured by a diver and ends up as a pet in the fish tank of a dentist in Sydney. Because of that, Marlin sets off on a journey to recover Nemo, enlisting the help of other creatures along the way. Until finally, Marlin and Nemo find each other, reunite, and learn that love depends on trust.

Here are three strategic planning stories that embrace the opportunity perspective:

Example I: *Once upon a time* there was a school district that wanted to ensure its students were completely prepared for the 21st century. *Every day*, staff would focus their time, energy, and effort on providing students technology, engaging projects, and opportunities to work in groups. *One day* the school district identified an opportunity to go deeper in developing core content knowledge required to perform many of the complex tasks and enhance their academic performance on various assessments. *Because of that*, everyone worked together to understand student performance and take action, involved students in the process of taking action over their learning, and took a more balanced approach to developing key knowledge and skills needed today and tomorrow. *Until finally*, every student was showing greater growth in their learning!

Example II: *Once upon a time* there was a school district that wanted to ensure its students were the top-performing students in the state. *Every day*, staff would focus their time, energy, and effort on preparing students to learn the content knowledge needed to have a competitive advantage. *One day* the school district found that students were looking for a greater level of engagement and involvement with the school, staff, and peers. *Because of that*, everyone worked together to find ways to engage learners in ways to work together to give and receive feedback and engaging in authentic problem solving. *Until finally*, every student was making more than one year's growth in one year's time and was engaged in the learning!

Example III: *Once upon a time* there was a school district that wanted to ensure students grew one year or more for each year of school. *Every day*, the director, principals, and staff would focus their time, energy, and effort on teacher clarity and student clarity. *One day*, the staff noticed an opportunity to connect strategy of clarity with greater ownership from the students about their learning, and with deeper learning experiences by the students. *Because of that*, everyone worked hard to find ways to develop and transfer leveled success criteria so as to engage students in their learning through deeper and more complex learning experiences. *Until finally*, every student was making more than one year's growth in one year's time and taking ownership over their learning.

Take your theory of action and embed it within the story frame. Next, get feedback from various stakeholders by asking the following questions.

- What is our simple message?
- What is unexpected about your message/solution? What is concrete?
- What are our credible resources?
- What is emotional/compelling?
- If you were going to tweet about our story, what would be your 280-character message?

Establish a Routine of Continual Inspection

Lastly, continually review your theory of action in light of evidence. The lead learner should establish brief checkpoints that include key data points of what is known, identify potential inferences, and draft potential next steps (see the "What? So What?, Now What?" protocol above). The lead learners are constantly working with leaders, teachers, and community members to gauge evidence of learning; serving each learner; working together to understand potential reasons for current performance; and determining next steps. Stated differently, the lead learners consider the plan as a working document that requires constant input to understand current performance and determine next steps. These next steps may include adjustments to practice or celebration of current practice. Therefore, monitoring performance and developing new actions are part and parcel of the planning process.

CONCLUSION

Chapter 2 focused on clarifying the organization's purpose to ensure substantial growth in 20th- and 21st-century learning. Always remember to stay small and stay focused on what matters most and ensure your strategic plan is constantly inspected and changed when needed. To do this, ensure your team answers three fundamental questions: *Where are we going?*, *Where are we now?*, and *What's next?* Within each of these questions there are several recommended steps that enable a leader to stay focused on learning and learners.

The next two chapters focus the reader on developing coherence in curriculum, instruction, assessment, and personnel services to enable an organization to execute the defining elements of the planning process and optimize autonomy along the way. Chapter 5 articulates how to ensure people within the organization are prepared to move and continue to move the right work forward.

REFLECTION QUESTIONS

1. How does the planning process compare and contrast to your current process?

2. What steps would you take to ensure that your strategic plan was one page (OK, maybe two pages)?

3. What steps would you take to clarify what you are going to do or focus on versus what you are not going to do or focus on?

4. When reviewing the three fundamental questions (Where are we going?, Where are we now?, and What's next?), identify which steps seem to be the most challenging to conduct in your context. Conduct a SWOT analysis and identify the key aspects within and around your organization that may be creating that challenge. Additionally, see Chapter 5 for specific skills that may enable you and your team to engage in every step.

5. Do you view your current plan as a "living document" that focuses specifically on the learning of children? Do you have a routine process for inspecting your performance and making changes to your planning documents?

6. How would you cut your strategic plan by 80 percent and reduce the number of priorities to one or two?

ACTIVITIES

ACTIVITY 2.1: DEVELOPING A MESSAGE

The following activity supports leaders in finding relationships among ideas related to the purpose, approach, and actions of an organization.

- **Step I:** Send the following questions to a diverse team of people asking them to draft answers. Be prepared to share those ideas in a large-group setting and develop next steps to support the organization.

    Script excerpt: Imagine you are going to create three tweets (280 characters total) about your school that will be shared with the world. The first tweet describes the "why" of the school (Why does the school exist, and why does the school serve children and your community?). The second tweet describes "how" the school makes an impact on students (How does your school serve children and the community at large?). The final tweet describes the "what" of the school (What does the school do to serve children and the community and what does the school not do to serve children and the community?) What would you write? What would the executive team, staff, students, and parents write? Would you have coherence around your purpose?

- **Step II:** When you meet with the group, engage in the following:

  Allow everyone to share their first tweet (the "why" response). Once complete, ask the group to identify similarities in the message (typically keywords).

  Engage in the same process with the "how" responses (second tweet). This time ask people to identify the similarities in how the school approaches solving problems, meeting challenges, and seeking new opportunities.

  For the third question, ask the group to share their "what" responses (third tweet). This time let everyone know that they will have an opportunity to respond twice. The first response is related to what the organization does do or is anticipating doing. The second response is related to what the organization does not do and is not looking at doing. Place these responses in two columns on a large sheet of paper (one column: actions we take; second column: actions we do not take). Ask the respondents to identify what the differences are between the two columns.

- **Step III:** Ask the group to create three new tweets that bring together the key findings from the group's discussion.

  1. Identify your impact: Using the discrepancy analysis protocol (see Figure 2.8), identify the current state of affairs of the organization and identify next steps related to established outcomes. Next, engage in a SWOT analysis to articulate ways to support or modify the proposed next steps.

  2. Feedback via Prototype: Create a draft one-page plan that outlines the work for next year and get feedback immediately from as many stakeholder groups as possible. Engage in this process three or four times. Consider using one of the following protocols in the Appendix (#10: Critical Friends, #5: Constructivist Tuning Protocol).

ACTIVITY 2.2: SWOT ANALYSIS

The following protocol allows participants to evaluate strengths, weaknesses, opportunities, and threats that are critical for analyzing internal and external constraints.

Suggested Time: 45 minutes

Opening Moves (Introduction) (5 minutes)

- Review purpose of protocol.
- Review agreements (or norms) of the team.
- Identify facilitator/participant and participants.
- Post chart and label with the following words: "Strengths," "Weaknesses," "Opportunities," and "Threats." See Figure 2.11 for an exemplar.

Figure 2.11   SWOT Template

Strengths	Weaknesses
Opportunities	Threats

Statements of Problem/Challenge/Circumstance (10 minutes)

- Present the idea/challenge or circumstance.
- Discuss the need to identify potential strengths/weaknesses/opportunities/threats.
- Participants should form into small groups of 3 or 4.

Group Development (10 minutes)

- Groups begin developing ideas (typically on sticky notes) and including them under each of the four quadrants of the matrix.

Collective Group Discussion (10 minutes)

- Everyone comes back and discusses the following questions:

    ○ What key ideas stand out? What surprises you?
    ○ What inferences emerge? What themes and patterns emerge? What implications to our organization can we draw?
    ○ What can we do with this information? What next steps do you recommend?

ACTIVITY 2.3: GAP ANALYSIS

The following protocol allows participants to identify the differences between the desired outcome and current performance or actual state of affairs. As a leader, identify your key outcome and use the following protocol to identify your current status.

Suggested Time: 35 minutes

Opening Moves (Introduction) (5 minutes)

- Review purpose of protocol.
- Review agreements (or norms) of the team.
- Identify facilitator/participant and participants.

**Statements of Problem/Challenge/
Circumstance** (15 minutes)

- Ask participants to identify the idea, state, or outcome they are trying to reach. Provide a scenario, review reference documents, or offer a general description.
- Ask participants to define the actual or current state/performance level at this point in time.

Next Steps (15 minutes)

- Ask participants what can be done to alleviate the discrepancy between the ideal state and current state/performance level.
- Identify five key steps the organization could take now.

ACTIVITY 2.4: ETCHED IN SAND: INTEGRITY VS. FIDELITY

Often a strategic planning process can take weeks if not months, requiring multiple meetings with multiple stakeholders, before any actions in the school or district can take place. The resulting strategic plan can be hundreds of pages articulating the best of intentions. This six-step activity pushes lead learners to create a strategic plan while implementing the plan simultaneously. The idea is to learn through action and not be beholden to implementing a plan (i.e., not fidelity to a plan) and focusing more on the three key questions (i.e., integrity to learning) that drive the process:

Step I: Collect data from students across the system on the three fundamental questions: *Where are we going?*, *Where are we now?*, and *What's next?*

Step II: Bring the data to a small focus group and ask them if the responses from students mirror their expectations. Next, ask the group to come up with the responses they would like to see from students.

Step III: Support the focus group in identifying a theory of action. Next, ask them to identify a potential way of testing that theory of action in the next 3 to 4 weeks.

Step IV: Test the idea and gather data.

Step V: Share results with the focus group and conduct another focus group within a 1- to 2-week timeframe. Next, identify potential next steps and set up a meeting to discuss results in 4 to 8 weeks.

Step VI: Discuss results and repeat Step V.

NEXT STEPS

1. Engage in the activities mentioned above. Once completed, compare and contrast your previous planning documents, planning processes, and messaging to your current drafts. What appears to be the key differences in terms of clarity of message and connection with stakeholders? What similarities do you notice? How did your community handle articulating what you are not going to do?

2. Adopt the plan with your stakeholders and draft a calendar that includes opportunities for feedback and inspection of implementation and impact.

RESOURCE

RESOURCE 2.1: IT'S NOT ABOUT THE PROGRAM

In the following activity, identify the goal of the district, the criteria for success, and the program(s) that the district has identified for moving the learning forward. Next, identify how clear your department, school, or district is on the goal, success criteria, and programs in the district. Based on this response, what next steps will you take?

Goals of the District (i.e., the learning intentions)

- Students are engaged in the International Baccalaureate Program.
- Students are clear on core outcomes, current progress, and next steps in their learning.
- Teachers are providing instruction and feedback at the students' level of understanding (surface, deep, and transfer).
- Students will be able to show more than one year's growth in one year's time in core academic content and 21st-century skills.
- Students are deeply involved in AVID (advancement via individual determination) and effective direct instruction.
- Students participate in problem- and project-based learning in a STEAM (science, technology, engineering, the arts, and mathematics) based environment.

- Teachers are providing instruction based on specific student needs (English language development, cultural responsive pedagogy).
- Students are able to answer three fundamental questions: *Where am I going?*, *Where am I?*, and *What's next?*

Goals of the District (i.e., the learning intentions)

```



```

Success Criteria

```



```

Programs/Methods/Approaches

```



```

How clear is your staff on the goals of the district, success criteria, and programs/methods?

```



```

Solution

Goals of the District (i.e., the learning intentions)

- Students will be able to show more than one year's growth in one year's time in core academic content and 21st-century skills.

Success Criteria

- Teachers are providing instruction based on specific student needs (English language development, cultural responsive pedagogy).
- Students are able to answer three fundamental questions: *Where am I going?*, *Where am I?*, and *What's next?*
- Students are clear on core outcomes, current progress, and next steps in their learning.
- Teachers are providing instruction and feedback at the students' level of understanding (surface, deep, and transfer).

Programs/Methods/Approaches

- Students are engaged in the International Baccalaureate Program.
- Students are deeply involved in AVID (advancement via individual determination) and effective direct instruction.
- Students participate in problem- and project-based learning in a STEAM (science, technology, engineering, the arts, and mathematics) based environment.

3

Coherence (Part I)
Learning System Infrastructure

The central premise of *Moneyball: The Art of Winning an Unfair Game* (Lewis, 2003) is that the collective wisdom of baseball experts and "insiders" in the past century were constructed primarily by experience and, as a result, were found to be capricious in nature and rarely produced the results necessary to field a successful baseball team. Though some statistics were utilized in the past, they were found to be less impactful than expected as they tended to focus on the wrong influences. The Oakland A's, however, began to focus on statistics that identified a few key influences that made a substantial impact on player performance (e.g., on-base percentage) rather than less substantial indicators (e.g., off-field behavior).

More importantly, the analytical results were not just used in initial selection and evaluation, but in the development of players. Coaches, using statistical results, worked with players to develop their knowledge and skills. The statistics were part of a system of improvement rather than a "check off" list devoid of intuition, collaboration, and experience. This took time however, as DePodesta (one of the key leaders within the A's) remarked prior to a 2012 lecture: "We learned every year. We discovered where we were wrong. There were things we implemented in a simplistic or incredibly straightforward way. Ten years later, we laugh at how extreme those positions were . . . the data can go too far" (Fancher, 2013). They found a way to blend data with the clinical expertise of staff to influence an organization.

Education is now facing a similar renaissance. Ample evidence from the cullers of research (i.e., Robinson, Marzano, Hattie) have shown what makes a substantial difference on student learning. Even more, the research has shown that almost everything in education works (Hattie, 2009). What separates "what works" from "what works best" is that the latter focuses on the relentless effort of adults to enhance student learning by illuminating student prior knowledge and intervening accordingly and providing students the tools to understand and direct their own learning (see Figure 3.1). To put the influences in Figure 3.1 into perspective, a .40 effect size is approximately one year's growth in one year's time.

"What works" interventions predominantly require no real focused effort from adults in the school on the actual learning of children but rather structures—schedules, class size, funding, curriculum, technology, furniture, and uniforms. Almost a decade after the *Visible Learning* research was published, the "What works best" influences have remained at the top of the list of what makes an impact. Concurrently, research found that many of the "what worked" instructional strategies had a powerful effect on student learning at different levels of learning (i.e., surface, deep, and transfer). For example, problem-based learning has an effect size of .21 at

Figure 3.1   Sample of Influences Related to Impact: What Works? vs. What Works Best?

What works? Below .40	What works best? .40 and above
Homework (.29)	Assessment-capable learning
Multi-grade/age classes (.04)	(1.33)
School calendars/timetables (.09)	Feedback (.70)
Open vs. Traditional Classrooms	Collective teacher efficacy (1.57)
(.01)	Classroom discussion (.82)
Class size (.21)	Self-efficacy (.92)
Finance (.21)	Teacher clarity (.75)
Ability grouping (.12)	Seeking help with peers (.83)
Within-class grouping (.18)	Deliberate practice (.79)
Clickers (.22)	Concentration/persistence/
Use of PowerPoint (.26)	engagement (.56)
Problem-based learning (.21)	Help seeking (.60)
Discovery-based teaching (.21)	Direct instruction (.60)
Charter schools (.09)	Strategy monitoring (.58)
Co-/team teaching (.19)	Goals (.68)
Web-based learning (.19)	Planning and prediction (.76)
Morning vs. evening (.12)	Rehearsal and memorization (.73)
	Elaboration and organization (.75)

Source: McDowell, 2018. Data pulled from John Hattie, *Visible Learning,* 2009.

surface-level learning but nearly quadrupled when learners were at deeper and transfer level learning (Hattie & Donoghue, 2016).

The lead learner must balance the need for focusing on key influences that make a substantial impact on student learning and using data to measure performance with a high degree of flexibility in how staff uses data to celebrate and improve performance. As you will see, the lead learners design and scale criteria for effectiveness and promote maximum flexibility in strategy. This chapter focuses on how leaders develop the coherence necessary to focus on what works best with high levels of voice and choice.

Setting the Stage for Coherence

In the end, the ultimate criterion of educational success for a teacher, department, school, or larger district system is that a substantial change in student learning of content and 21st-century outcomes has occurred over an established period of time (e.g., over the course of a project/unit or an academic year). As Nuthall (2007) argues,

> Generally, effective teaching means students learn what you intend them to learn (or some part of what you intend). You may want them to acquire new knowledge and beliefs, new skills or different attitudes, or some mixture of all of these. But whatever you intend, in order to know if you have been effective, you must have some way of knowing what your students believed, knew, could do, or felt before you taught them and what your students believed, knew, could do, or felt after you taught them. Learning, of whatever kind, is about change, and unless you know what has changed in the minds, skills, and attitudes of your students, you cannot really know how effective you have been. (p. 35)

As a result, the lead learners must anchor their systems' overall decision-making on the progress and proficiency of student learning across levels of complexity (surface, deep, and transfer) in the areas of core academic content and 21st-century skills. To build such a system, lead learners must (1) establish growth and proficiency expectations and (2) establish standardized and customizable features to support staff in moving learning forward for all children.

Establish Progress and Proficiency Expectations

To begin such efforts, educators (and students) must develop a common understanding of levels of learning. There are a number of ways to define a hierarchy of learning. This text recommends using the following approach:

1. **Surface:** A student understands ideas and/or skills in isolation.

2. **Deep:** A student relates ideas and/or skills.

3. **Transfer:** A student applies ideas/and or skills in different situations.

Educators (and students) must also have a standard way to delineate performance levels that are deemed proficient and to create a standard measure of adequate growth in learning over time. One suggestion is for students and teachers to use a 0.0–4.0 scale to match learning levels and designate a proficiency level (such as 3.0 or above) to be at the deep/transfer level of learning for students (see Figure 3.2). This designation would allow educators and students to clearly delineate student performance levels and effectively provide targeted support.

Figure 3.2 Levels of Learning

SUCCESS CRITERIA	SCORE	
Transfer Applying Understanding	4.0	• **Met transfer expectations**
	3.5	• **Partially met transfer expectations**
Deep Making Meaning	3.0	• **Met deep expectations**
	2.5	• **Partially met deep expectations**
Surface Building Knowledge	2.0	• **Met single/multiple expectations**
	1.5	• **Partial success with single/multiple expectations**

SUCCESS CRITERIA	SCORE	
With Support	1.0	• **With instructional support, student met single/multiple and relational expectations.**
	0.5	• **With instructional support, student met single/multiple level expectations.**
	0.0	• **With instructional support, student has not met single/multiple level expectations.**

Source: McDowell, M. P. (2017). *Rigorous PBL by design.* Thousand Oaks, CA: Corwin.

In addition to determining student proficiency ranges, school systems need to identify a standardized way to determine the amount of progress students have made over a given period of time. Effect sizes are a powerful way of determining student growth over time. Based on the *Visible Learning* research, educators can relate the effect sizes of their students to the "hinge point." The hinge point denotes one year's growth in one year's time. Interestingly, this reference point also denotes the potential impact instructional practices would have on student learning. As Hattie (2011) states,

> Setting the bar at an effect size of d = 0.0 is so low as to be dangerous. We need to be more discriminating. For any particular intervention to be considered worthwhile, it needs to show an improvement in student learning of at least an average gain—that is, an effect size of at least 0.40. The d = 0.40 is what I referred to in Visible Learning as the hinge-point (or h-point) for identifying what is and what is not effective. (pp. 2–3)

This text recommends using the .40 effect size as a way to determine whether students are getting one year's growth in one year's time (and as we will discuss later, it should be used to discriminate strategies teachers are selecting to move learning forward).

Once educators have established standard progress and proficiency levels and a standard set of complexity levels, schools and school systems are much more likely to effectively prepare, implement, and respond to student learning. Figure 3.3 illustrates how a system may integrate the ideas of progress, proficiency, and levels of learning. Figure 3.4 articulates students' performance at each level.

Figure 3.3   Progress and Proficiency Across Levels of Complexity Matrix

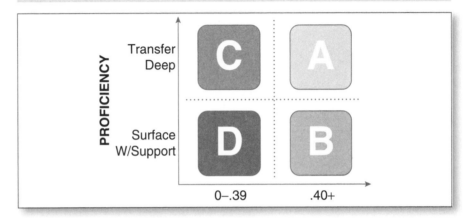

Figure 3.4   Description of Student Performance

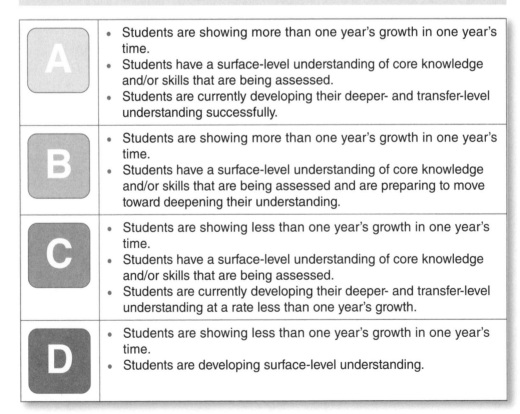

A	• Students are showing more than one year's growth in one year's time. • Students have a surface-level understanding of core knowledge and/or skills that are being assessed. • Students are currently developing their deeper- and transfer-level understanding successfully.
B	• Students are showing more than one year's growth in one year's time. • Students have a surface-level understanding of core knowledge and/or skills that are being assessed and are preparing to move toward deepening their understanding.
C	• Students are showing less than one year's growth in one year's time. • Students have a surface-level understanding of core knowledge and/or skills that are being assessed. • Students are currently developing their deeper- and transfer-level understanding at a rate less than one year's growth.
D	• Students are showing less than one year's growth in one year's time. • Students are developing surface-level understanding.

Establish Standardized and Customizable Features

Based on the ever-changing dynamics of the classrooms and schools, lead learners realize that each school, department or grade-level team, and individual teacher need to have autonomy to make key decisions to move student learning forward. At the same time, lead learners need to make sure that all schools have the tools necessary to identify and take action on student progress and proficiency at defined levels of complexity. This text argues that the standardization of progress and proficiency provides a greater level of customization in the field. The lead learners meet these expectations by juxtaposing standardized criteria and customizable approaches (see Figure 3.5) in the following areas: (1) learning intentions and success criteria and (2) targeted instruction.

Develop Learning Intentions and Success Criteria

Educational research has shown time and time again that when students are clear on the goals or intentions of learning and understand what success looks like in meeting those goals, students learn at a substantial level. In fact, student clarity doubles the rate of learning and is essential for effective feedback (which happens to also double the rate of learning). Moreover, students have a far greater chance of developing the knowledge and skills to take more responsibility over their own learning if they know what is expected in their learning.

Based on the systematic work that lead learners have done to clarify levels of learning, learning intentions and success criteria

Figure 3.5   Standardized and Customizable Components

A quality learning system will include the following standardized components:	A quality learning system will include the following customizable components:
• Common learning intentions and success criteria for students • Criteria for approaches to teaching that increase learning	• Customizable approaches to supporting students in understanding and meeting expectations • Customizable approaches to teaching students at varying levels of complexity

should be used to clarify these levels to everyone and should be consistent across each school and each grade level. In other words, no matter what teacher a student gets at a grade level or course, the learning intentions and success criteria should be the same.

Simultaneously, learning intentions and success criteria should maximize autonomy for teachers in every classroom. Notice in Figures 3.6 and 3.7 that the success criteria are devoid of tasks, activities, and context. Nor do these figures articulate the way to assess student learning or how to teach to those intentions and success criteria.

Ultimately, this approach provides teachers the option to select the best way to assess student learning, identify the best activities and resources to use, and determine the best instructional approach and the situation or context of the lesson/unit.

Figure 3.6   Example Scale for Content—Biology Example

Success Criteria	Score	Description
Transfer Applying Understanding	4.0	• Designs and conducts an experiment to predict how cells change in various situations
	3.5	
Deep Making Meaning	3.0	• Cites research-based and own evidence that verifies premise that cells are living and differ from nonliving things • Draws conclusions about how cells function through experimentation
	2.5	
Surface Building Knowledge	2.0	• Classifies organelle functions within a cell • Summarizes the key aspects of living things
	1.5	
With Support	1.0	
	.5	
	0.0	

Figure 3.7   Example Scale for Skills—Mathematical Practices Example

	Learning intentions	Surface Success Criteria 0————2.0	Deep Success Criteria 2.5————3.0	Transfer Success Criteria 3.5————4.0
1a	Make sense of problems.	Explain thought processes in solving a problem one way.	Explain thought processes in solving a problem and representing it in several ways.	Discuss, explain, and demonstrate solving a problem with multiple representations in multiple ways.
1b	Persevere in solving them.	Stay with a challenging problem for more than one attempt.	Try several approaches in finding a solution, and only seek hints if stuck.	Struggle with various attempts over time, and learn from previous solution attempts.
2	Reason abstractly and quantitatively.	Reason with models or pictorial.	Are able to translate situations into symbols for solving problems.	Convert situations into symbols as well as convert symbols into meaningful situations.
3a	Construct viable arguments.	Explain thinking for the solution found.	Explain their own thinking and thinking of others with accurate vocabulary.	Justify and explain, with accurate language and vocabulary, why their solution is correct.
3b	Critique the reasoning of others.	Understand and discuss other ideas and approaches.	Explain other students' solutions and identify strengths and weaknesses of the solution.	Compare and contrast various solution strategies and explain the reasoning of others.
4	Model with mathematics.	Use models to represent and solve a problem, and translate the solution to mathematical symbols.	Use models and symbols to represent and solve a problem, and accurately explain the solution representation.	Use of a variety of models, symbolic representations, and technology tools to demonstrate a solution to a problem.

(Continued)

Figure 3.7 (Continued)

	Learning intentions	Surface Success Criteria 0———2.0	Deep Success Criteria 2.5———3.0	Transfer Success Criteria 3.5———4.0
5	Use appropriate tools strategically.	Use the appropriate tool to find a solution.	Select from a variety of tools to solve a problem, and explain reasoning for the selection.	Combine various tools, including technology, to explore and solve a problem as well as justify their tool selection and problem solution.
6	Attend to precision.	Communicate their reasoning and solution to others.	Incorporate appropriate vocabulary and symbols when communicating with others.	Use appropriate symbols, vocabulary, and labeling to effectively communicate and exchange ideas.
7	Look for and make use of structure.	Look for structure within mathematics to help them solve problem efficiently.	Compose and decompose number situations and relationships through observed patterns in order to simplify solutions.	See complex and complicated mathematical expressions as component parts.
8	Look for and express regularity in repeated reasoning.	Look for obvious patterns, and use if/then reasoning strategies for obvious patterns.	Find and explain subtle patterns.	Discover deep, underlying relationships (i.e., uncover a model or equation that unifies the various aspects of a problem such as discovering an underlying function).

Develop Targeted Instructional Support

The lead learners are tasked with developing an instructional model for school systems that offers instructional, feedback, and learning strategies that research and "in practice" results have shown to have a high probability of impact at the surface, deep, and transfer levels.

Research has illustrated that a "fit" exists between the strategies teachers and students use at each level of learning (Hattie & Donoghue, 2016; Hattie & Timperley, 2007; Marzano, 2017). Figure 3.8 illustrates instructional, feedback, and learning strategies at all levels of complexity

Figure 3.8   Instructional, Feedback, and Learning Strategies Coherence to Levels of Learning

Learning Progression		Surface	Deep	Transfer
		Understands one concept, idea, and/or skill	Understands how concepts, ideas, and skills relate	Understands how to transfer concepts and relationships between concepts to various contexts
Instructional Strategies	*Effective teaching strategies to enable students to develop understanding of core knowledge or skill*	• Previewing new content (KWL, advanced organizer) • Chunking content into "digestible bites" (e.g., the teacher presents content in smaller portions) • Elaborating one new information (e.g., the teacher asks questions that require students to make and defend inferences) • Recording and representing knowledge	• Examining similarities and differences (e.g., the teacher engages students in comparing, classifying, creating analogies and metaphors) • Examining errors in reasoning (e.g., the teacher asks students to examine fallacies, propaganda, and bias)	• Engaging students in cognitively complex tasks (e.g., the teacher engages students in decision-making tasks, problem-solving tasks, investigative tasks) • Providing resources and guidance (e.g., the teacher makes resources available)

(Continued)

Figure 3.8 (Continued)

Learning Progression		Surface	Deep	Transfer
Feedback Strategies	*Effective forms of feedback to enable students to move forward in their learning*	Provide information to students that helps them think through the tasks at hand by • distinguishing correct from incorrect answer, • acquiring more or different information, and • building more surface knowledge.	Provide information to students that helps them process • relationships between ideas, and • finding ways to detect errors in thinking and engaging in activities.	Provide information to students that helps them self-regulate their learning by • creating ways to self-assess performance, • forming strategies to seek support in learning, and • monitoring and investing in seeking and acting on feedback to improve.
Learning Strategies	*Effective strategies students may use to assist them in their own learning*	• outlining • mnemonics • summarization • underlining and highlighting • note-taking • deliberate practice • rehearsal	• seeking help from peers • classroom discussions • evaluation and reflection • self-verbalization and self-questioning • metacognitive strategies	• identifying similarities and differences in problems • seeing patterns in new situations

Source: McDowell, M. P. (2017). *Rigorous PBL by design.* Thousand Oaks, CA: Corwin.

that a system could use to support teachers in identifying an appropriate intervention for student learning.

Coherence: Bringing It All Together

Once systems have developed a standard approach to progress, proficiency, and a standard language and expectations of complexity, educators and students are able to analyze performance and make targeted adjustments. Providing learning intentions and success criteria as well as an ever-evolving instructional model gives teachers the tools to make instructional decisions that have a high probability of making a substantial impact on learning. Figure 3.9 illustrates potential approaches teachers could take if all these elements are in place in their school, department, or grade level. Lead learners ensure these elements are in place so that teachers make accurate and autonomy decisions that substantially move learning forward.

Figure 3.9   Potential Approach to Intervention

	Students are demonstrating high proficiency (surface, deep, and transfer understanding) and are showing more than one year's growth in their learning. Potential interventions include: • *Instructional Strategies: Provide new contexts to similar content and/or add new layers of content to challenge learner.* • *Feedback Strategies: Support students in developing their capacity to find new ways to give and receive feedback on their learning.* • *Learning Strategies: Reflect on strategies that moved learning forward.*
	Students are demonstrating low proficiency (surface understanding) and are showing more than one year's growth in their learning. Potential interventions include: • *Instructional Strategies: Use jigsaw and interleaving to support students in moving from surface to deep learning (involve students in the "C" category as well).* • *Feedback Strategies: Give students sample work to detect errors and explore new learning strategies.* • *Learning Strategies: Use success criteria to review others' work and give and receive feedback.*
	Students are demonstrating high proficiency (surface, deep, and transfer understanding) and are showing less than one year's growth in their learning. Potential interventions include: • *Instructional Strategies: Provide complex cognitively challenging tasks for students (e.g., investigative tasks, problem-solving tasks).* • *Feedback Strategies: Support students in self-assessing their performance and identifying next steps in their learning.* • *Learning Strategies: Identify similarities and differences in problems (i.e., understanding the underlying principles and the differences across contexts).*

(Continued)

Figure 3.9   (Continued)

Students are demonstrating low proficiency (surface understanding) and are showing less than one year's growth in their learning. Potential interventions include:

- *Instructional Strategies: Focus on students elaborating on ideas and recording information to support chunking of ideas.*
- *Feedback Strategies: Provide direct right/wrong feedback that enables learners to discern facts and skills.*
- *Learning Strategies: Directly teach outlining and using mnemonics in context.*

VOICES FROM THE FIELD

Chrysta Carlin, Executive Director of Secondary Curriculum

Leander ISD

Leander, Texas

I often rely on defined autonomy as a way to balance the instruction and transformation in a school or district. With the leadership team, we set high expectations for quality teaching and learning and give the teachers and campuses the autonomy of how to reach those expectations.

To maintain a focus on quality teaching and learning, teachers need to know their content, their students, and their data. While we often think of these three items as more of a traditional framework of education, they are important in building a solid foundation for transformational teaching and learning. As a campus staff, we built a vision for transformational learning for our school, then created a pathway for how to reach our vision. This pathway included the basics of quality teaching such as deep content knowledge, formative assessments, data analysis, best practices, and instructional strategies.

Eventually, we built on the foundation and moved to more authentic learning experiences for our students. We incorporated future-ready skills such as communication, collaboration, and creativity. Project-based learning (PBL) became the primary model of instruction on the campus, but we never lost sight of the basics. Our goal was to build a culture of academics that prepares students for their future. This required our teachers to get out of their comfort zone in regard to instruction and transform the learning experiences for our students to make it more meaningful.

As the campus leader, I worked with the leadership team to implement our own formative assessments on the learning experiences of our students. We often had the students and staff complete culture surveys to make sure the atmosphere in the school lent itself to a transformational learning environment where students had input into their learning experiences. We also checked the rigor of the courses to ensure students were learning at high levels and applying the learning in authentic settings. Based on this feedback, we provided the teachers with ongoing professional development in their content areas as well as in instructional methodologies such as PBL.

Now, as a district leader who oversees curriculum, it is important that our written curriculum includes the basics of unpacking our standards, clear student expectations, and tiered instructional strategies to meet the needs of all students. In addition, the documents must include examples of performance assessments and ideas for authentic learning as a means of helping teachers establish a need for students to learn the content and provide a more meaningful learning experience for all students. Our team must also provide a variety of professional learning for teachers to ensure we meet their needs regardless of where they are on the spectrum of instructional to transformational teachers. We must set the vision for teaching and learning and then support all teachers and campuses on reaching the vision.

CONCLUSION

The heart of a strong learning system is to "know thy impact" so that a system can determine individual and collective efficacy and take action. The lead learner defines *impact* by using progress and proficiency standards against levels of learning in core academic content and 21st-century skills. These leaders create coherence by supporting educators in operationalizing this work by creating common learning intentions and success criteria and maximizing professional judgment in how they are used in the classroom. Moreover, lead learners create (and continually develop) an instructional model that illuminates high-impact practices from the research and within the system that substantially move learning forward.

We will see in later chapters that the key to moving learning forward for students is the incessant actions of teachers (and learners!), constantly evaluating their impact on student learning growth, reviewing performance, and taking action in light of such evidence. But first, the right people need to be there and as such personnel systems must be aligned and utilized according to those beliefs and behaviors that make a substantial impact on children. Aligning beliefs and behaviors is critical, and in the next chapter we will explore a process for identifying new teachers for an educational system, providing targeted professional development, and creating evaluative systems that improve current employees along the novice to expert continuum.

REFLECTION QUESTIONS

1. As a lead learner, where do you have coherence and where do you allow or promote autonomy and/or divergence?

2. How does your school or school system define progress, proficiency, and levels of learning? How are these definitions different than what is described here?

3. How do the standardized features maximize customizable features schools, teacher teams, and individual teachers?

4. How do learning intentions and success criteria relate to the expectations your team provides to students across your system?

5. What are the areas that appear to be manageable to develop in the next six months to one year? What areas appear to be the most challenging? Why?

ACTIVITIES

ACTIVITY 3.1: IDENTIFYING KEY LEARNING INTENTIONS AND SUCCESS CRITERIA

Create small groups of teachers to categorize key outcomes that must be attained by students at the transfer level (i.e., "essential" outcomes), outcomes that are important to know and engage with but not necessary at the transfer level (i.e., "desirable" outcomes), and outcomes that are not necessary at the deep level (i.e., "Exposure" outcomes). See Figure 3.10.

Figure 3.10   Essential, Desirable, and Exposure Outcomes

Essential	Desirable	Exposure
• Outcomes that require students to learn surface-, deep-, and transfer-level knowledge and skills	• Outcomes that require students to learn surface- and deep-level knowledge and skills	• Outcomes that require students to learn surface-level knowledge and skills

To assist teachers in identifying essential learning intentions, this text recommends that teams evaluate and critique their outcomes using the questions in Figure 3.11. Next, have teachers create success criteria for each "essential" learning outcome. To do this, have teachers write out the learning intention in Figure 3.12 and begin populating success criteria at the surface, deep, and transfer levels. (Activity 3.2 walks leaders through a process for engaging in this work.)

Figure 3.11 **Characteristics/Questions**

Characteristics	Questions
Endurance	Will the outcome provide students with the knowledge and skills that are necessary beyond a specific test date?
Leverage	Will the outcome provide knowledge and skills that are necessary in other disciplines?
Focus	Will the learning outcome provide the knowledge and skills that are necessary within the next several grade levels in the discipline?
Redundancy	Will this learning outcome re-emerge in subsequent units and courses?

Figure 3.12 **Learning Intention and Success Criteria Template**

Surface	Deep	Transfer

Here is an example:

Example I: Core Academic Knowledge/Skill

Figure 3.13 **Learning Intention: I will initiate and participate effectively in a range of collaborative discussions (ELA Common Core Standard).**

Surface	Deep	Transfer
• Articulates evidence from a text • Paraphrases the comments from others • Identifies own ideas when speaking	• Relates others ideas' with their own when speaking in a range of collaborative discussions (one on one, in groups, and teacher led) • Relates evidence from texts with own ideas	• Applies several conversational strategies in various contexts

ACTIVITY 3.2: PROTOTYPE DEVELOPMENT: FOCUS AND FLARE

The following activity pushes educators to create multiple prototypes of content, conative, and cognitive learning intentions and success criteria via rubrics. To initiate this process, engage in the following steps:

- **Step I (Flare):** Establish several groups of teachers (e.g., Group A, Group B, Group C, and Group D) and have each group of teachers create several draft rubrics for several different learning intentions. [20 minutes]

- **Step II (Focus):** Have each group of teachers provide feedback to another group on the draft rubrics (e.g., Group A gives feedback to Group B and vice versa). [20 minutes]

- **Step III (Flare and Focus):** The groups engage in the process again using the feedback received. Next the groups give feedback to each other. Groups should find a different group to receive feedback (e.g., Group A gives feedback to Group C and vice versa).

- **Step IV (Field Test):** The groups go out and implement with students and bring back feedback to the larger group on next steps.

Figure 3.14   Focus and Flare

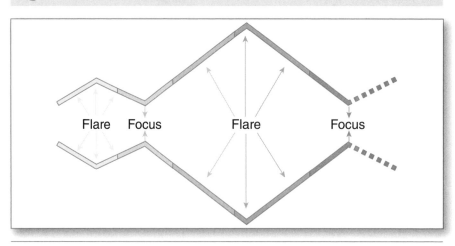

Source: Hasso Platner Institute of Design at Stanford (rendering by Jennifer Hennesy).

ACTIVITY 3.3: BUILD A RUBRIC

Learning Intention: I will understand and interact with others: Controversy and Conflict Resolution

Figure 3.15   21st-Century Rubric Samples

Success Criteria	Score	Description
Transfer Applying Understanding	4.0	• Applies multiple strategies in complex authentic situations • Formulates new strategies to enhance relationships
	3.5	
Deep Making Meaning	3.0	• Solves problems or de-escalates situations using more than one strategy
	2.5	
Surface Building Knowledge	2.0	• Can give examples and non-examples of effective strategies to address controversy and conflict • Performs the use of strategies in structured situations
	1.5	
With Support	1.0	
	.5	
	0.0	

Learning Intention: I will address complex problems and issues: Divergent and Convergent Thinking.

Figure 3.16   21st-Century Rubric

Success Criteria	Score	Description
Transfer Applying Understanding	4.0	• Applies convergent and divergent strategies to authentic, complex problems • Reflects on efficacy of implementation of strategies to solve complex problems
	3.5	
Deep Making Meaning	3.0	• Compares and contrasts the basic purposes and functions of convergent and divergent thinking • Relates convergent and divergent strategies to problems
	2.5	

(Continued)

Figure 3.16   (Continued)

Success Criteria	Score	Description
Surface Building Knowledge	2.0	• Matches convergent and divergent strategies to presented problems • Explains how various convergent and divergent strategies work
	1.5	
With Support	1.0	
	.5	
	0.0	

ACTIVITY 3.4: DESIGNING FOR TRANSFER—QUICKLY!

Work with teachers to develop rapid prototypes of units that focus on ensuring that students will be able to articulate learning intentions and understand levels of complexity via success criteria, and ensure that there is a high probability that the right strategies are being used to move all learners forward. Have teachers use the following planning template from *Rigorous PBL by Design* (McDowell, 2017) to create five units in an hour. Once that has been completed, have them give each other feedback using one of the protocols in the Appendix section of this book (e.g., #10 Critical Friends, #5 Constructivist Tuning Protocol).

Figure 3.17   Project Template

Project Design			
Step 1: Learning Intention(s)			
Step 2: Success Criteria			
	Surface	Deep	Transfer
Step 3: Driving Question(s)			
Context			

Project Design			
Step 4: Tasks			
	Surface	Deep	Transfer
Step 5: Entry Event			
	Scenario . . . Expectations . . . Patron . . . Format . . .		
Workshops			
	Surface	Deep	Transfer

Project Calendar					
	Monday	Tuesday	Wednesday	Thursday	Friday
Week 1 [Phase 1 and Phase 2]					
Week 2 [Phase 2 and Phase 3]					
Week 3 [Phase 3 and Phase 4]					

Source: McDowell, 2017.

ACTIVITY 3.5: THE END IN MIND

Using the Unit Template in the back of the book, have teachers review only the success criteria from the unit. Next, have teachers attempt to identify the learning intention. Repeat this process with other units/lessons and consider giving either the learning intention and having them create the success criteria or give them the success criteria and have them create the learning intention. This activity is helpful in supporting teachers in gaining clarity of expectations and giving and receiving feedback early on in the planning process.

NEXT STEPS

1. Identify key learning intentions and success criteria for each grade level and course across the system.

2. Develop rubrics for each learning intention and success criteria for each conative, cognitive, and content-based skill. Ensure that each rubric includes the levels of learning: surface, deep, and transfer.

4

Coherence (Part II)

Ensuring Inspired and Passionate Teachers in Schools

Think back to that teacher who believed in you, tapped into your passions, and prepared you for life. My first great teacher was actually an elementary school librarian who, for one reason or another, saw my passion for geography and continued to find time to show me books, listen to my stories, and provide me with guidance to continually read and write about my ideas of the world. My father was in the military, and I was incessantly curious about the places he was living in—What was food like? What did the country look like? Was it similar to the rural plains of Oklahoma?

I'm fortunate to have had Ms. Webb as a teacher because my first-grade teacher was quite the opposite of Ms. Webb. I asked her if we studied geography in first grade and she told me we would not have time for subjects like that. When we were tasked with conducting speed tests in mathematics, I asked if we could not use an egg timer as it was distracting. She put the egg timer on my desk for the entire year. I'm so fortunate that I had a mother who ensured I went into second grade, but I now know that who is with you when you are a captive audience makes a fundamental difference in your confidence, competence, and curiosity—and who you got as a teacher appeared to be a lottery.

Learning is an immensely social enterprise composed of relationships, guidance, and support. As such, people are the fundamental building block of education. One teacher (or one leader for that matter) can make a substantial impact on a student; multiple teachers can arguably solidify someone's trajectory in life. The role of the lead learner is to design a system that continuously recruits, selects, and develops educators that focus on substantially causing learning for every learner. This chapter focuses on coherence of our human resource approach to ensure the right people are in place. In the end, it will never be structures, systems, or processes that make the impact (though they greatly help); it will always be people.

Linking Learner-Centered Beliefs and Behaviors

As discussed earlier, contemporary research found that almost everything we do in education makes an impact; in essence, everything works. The influences that make the greatest impact consistently relate to teachers' beliefs and their practices. The link between key beliefs and behaviors has been studied in numerous texts and is, perhaps, most vividly expressed in Anthony Muhammad's (2009) bestselling book, *Transforming School Culture: How to Overcome Staff Division*, where he outlined specific archetypes of educators that are characteristic of typical teachers in America. Of these archetypes, the two most prevalent and impactful are fundamentalists and believers. Figure 4.1 outlines these archetypes by definition and illustrates similarities and differences in belief systems.

A cursory view of Figure 4.1 illuminates to leaders how *critical* it is to unmask the difference between these teacher types as student achievement, motivation, and long-term performance depend on it. Lead learners must therefore construct a system that accurately

Figure 4.1 Educator Typology

Similarities	Differences
(1) Both believers and fundamentalists like kids, want to work with kids, and want kids to be successful. (2) Both believers and fundamentalists can be highly skilled in the art and science of teaching.	(1) Only believers think that all kids can learn and learn at high levels and that the teachers, school leaders, and school staff are responsible for moving student learning to high levels. Fundamentalists do not see this as their responsibility.

selects and develops educators that believe they can and will *cause* learning for all children. They do this by linking the beliefs and behaviors that have been shown to have the greatest impact on student learning to a human resources system. Figure 4.2 shows high-impact teacher and leadership beliefs that have a high probability of making a substantial impact on student learning (Hattie, 2012).

Figure 4.2   High-Impact Teacher and Leadership Beliefs

1	Teachers/leaders believe that their fundamental task is to evaluate the effect of their teaching on students' learning and achievement.
2	Teachers/leaders believe that success and failure in student learning is about what they, as teachers or leaders, did or did not do. We are change agents.
3	Teachers/leaders want to talk more about the learning than the teaching.
4	Teachers/leaders see assessment as feedback about their impact.
5	Teachers/leaders engage in dialogue, not monologue.
6	Teachers/leaders enjoy the challenge and never retreat to "doing their best."
7	Teachers/leaders believe that it is their role to develop positive relationships in classrooms/staffrooms.
8	Teachers/leaders inform all about the language of learning.
9	Teachers/leaders inform all about how learning is hard work.
10	Teachers/leaders collaborate with others on a routine basis to influence learning.

Source: McDowell, 2018. Data pulled from John Hattie, *Visible Learning,* 2009.

Figure 4.3 separates these beliefs into two categories: (a) *Relational*—those beliefs that are centered on ensuring that a trusting and supportive connection between teachers and *all* students is developed and sustained, and (b) *Tactical*—those beliefs that are centered on using the professional technical knowledge and skills of a teacher to ensure students are learning at high levels in 21st-century skills (including conative skills—self- and social awareness and management—and cognitive critical-thinking and problem-solving knowledge and skills) and content-based outcomes.

Figure 4.3 Relational and Tactical Beliefs

Relational	Tactical
• "We are change agents" • Talk more about learning than teaching • Engage in dialogue not monologue • Enjoy the challenge • Positive relationships • Sees learning as challenging • I collaborate	• Evaluate the effects of their teaching • Assessment as feedback regarding their impact • Inform all about the language of learning • I collaborate

Unmasking Beliefs and Behaviors

Imagine an interview where the main questions that were asked to a candidate related specifically to their affinity toward children and their use of an array of instructional practices. In this way, both groups (i.e., believers and fundamentalists) could feasibly shine in the interview. Imagine an evaluation process where there is one main observation that is related to implementing a lesson plan or using a variety of instructional strategies; both groups theoretically could perform well. However, how would fundamentalists and believers perform if they were given student performance data and asked how they would respond? Fundamentalists would likely assign responsibility to children, outside school forces, or working conditions. Believers would likely focus efforts on improving their own practices, finding others to collaborate with to support student learning, and talking with children to find out what worked and what didn't.

Even more challenging, research has shown repeatedly that what we say is not necessarily equivalent to what we do in reality. As Schwarz (2013) states, "The problem is that in challenging situations, the mindset leaders use is rarely the one they think they are using" (p. 6). In essence, a hidden philosophy exists within us, which is inherently linked to a set of behaviors that are expressed routinely in challenging situations. Teachers and leaders are met with challenges daily and therefore express certain behaviors, derived from their hidden philosophy, ubiquitously and voluminously throughout their daily lives. How do leaders then identify, support, and evaluate educators based on the right beliefs and the right behaviors day to day when they may not tell us?

First, we need to get out of our own way. Leaders (as do all humans) carry a substantial number of biases (see Figure 4.4) that greatly influence

Figure 4.4 Influential Human Biases

Bias	Description
Loss aversion	People's tendency to prefer avoiding losses to acquiring equivalent gain
Value attribution	Describes our tendency to imbue people or objects with certain qualities based on perceived value, rather than on objective data
Diagnosis bias	Refers to our propensity to label people, ideas, or objects based on our initial opinions of them—and our inability to reconsider these judgments once we have made them
Overconfidence	Refers to our high level of confidence in our judgment relative to the facts

our decisions, and this is most vividly on display and has some of the greatest consequences when people are engaged in hiring.

The biases in Figure 4.4 work collectively to persuade our judgments and often lead to faulty hiring and evaluation decisions.

Though research has shown that we are heavily biased in our hiring and evaluation practices, many people would fight to counter this notion because the process used in most schools and districts are comfortable and routine. Gladwell (2000) sums up these biases at play in the hiring process well:

For most of us, hiring someone is essentially a romantic process, in which the job interview functions as a desexualized version of a date. We are looking for someone with whom we have a certain chemistry, even if the coupling that results ends in tears and the pursuer and the pursued turn out to have nothing in common. We want the unlimited promise of a love affair. The structured interview, by contrast, seems to offer only the dry logic and practicality of an arranged marriage. (p. 85)

People believe they are using rational processes and decision-making when often they are actually thinking with their gut. The hiring process may best be compared to a round of speed dating as our infatuations (or lack thereof) of people are determined within the first few seconds of an interview. Our evaluation processes may be best compared to a "dog and pony" show: evaluations are typically over-staged presentations designed to convince others of their teaching performance (regardless of their views on learning or how they respond when students show variations in their own learning). Wiliam (2016) found that our reliability and validity with teacher observations and overall effectiveness were completely arbitrary due to various biases.

In sum, the differences in belief systems that matter are less intuitive than we think (e.g., often educators with inappropriate belief systems can still possess high skill), what people say and what they do in the classroom are not aligned, and there are a number of biases that influence people when making decisions that can influence hiring, professional development (as discussed in the next chapter), and evaluations. Lead learners need to find and evaluate teachers with these challenges in mind.

We cannot rely on our gut when it comes to who we put in front of our children nor make massive inferences in a single observation. We can *never* give into quality when it comes to ensuring our most vulnerable and prized resource—our children—have caring, determined, highly effective educators with them. You may be "hooked on a feeling" but that feeling may cost the curiosity, competence, and confidence of our children.

Hiring and Developing Educators for Impact

To ensure that the hiring and educator development process is predictive of high impact on student learning, the message is *always* hire and evaluate for impact on learning. Lead learners engage in hiring and personnel development by ensuring teachers have the right beliefs and behaviors to make an impact on student and staff learning and that educators are receiving the right supports to move their learning forward. Figure 4.5 lays out three key areas of focus: beliefs, behaviors, and building capacity. This chapter focuses on the first two elements, while the following chapter articulates the process leaders take to build staff capacity.

Lead learners take the following steps to ensure the right educators and the right supports are in place for all children:

- Articulate expectations
- Filter candidates
- Engage in structured interviews
- Conduct general interviews and demonstrations
- Provide targeted feedback and support

Figure 4.5 Three Elements of the Personnel Logic Model

Beliefs Defining, filtering, and selecting high-impact educators	Leader focuses on identifying the right beliefs of each candidate and whether each candidate expresses such beliefs in typical classroom and professional culture situations.
Behaviors Exploring and identifying expertise of a potential high-impact educator	Leader focuses on identifying if the right behaviors are in place for developing strong relationships with children and colleagues as well as using the practices that enable students to learn at high levels in content and 21st-century skills (i.e., conative and cognitive knowledge and skills).
Building capacity of educators	Leader focuses on identifying if educators are showing high levels of growth in moving student learning forward and moving their own learning forward as a professional. This step also focuses on feedback and collectively developing next steps to celebrate successes, seek new opportunities to learn, and improve.

Step 1: Articulate Expectations

Figures 4.1 and 4.2 lay out the specific beliefs that are found in the literature to make a substantial impact on all children at all levels of learning. Once a clear definition of the beliefs and expected actions has been developed, administrators must find a way to identify if those beliefs play out in specific situations. These beliefs (and associated actions) should be clearly articulated in job descriptions (see Figure 4.6) and evaluation forms.

Figure 4.6 Job Description

Job Description

The role of a teacher within the _____ School is to serve each learner and substantially impact the learning of all children. As such, teachers must believe all students can learn at high levels and that they as teachers are a causal agent of such learning and must possess a repertoire of instructional skills to create an atmosphere that inspires learning and target instruction to support each learner in progressing toward key learning outcomes.

(Continued)

Figure 4.6 (Continued)

The teacher is directly responsible for utilizing assessment and instructional practices that substantially enhance student learning within his or her classroom, and across the school, and create an engaging and respectful learning environment. The position entails evaluating assessment data, designing classroom instruction, establishing and maintaining a positive classroom culture, and working closely with students and teachers to measure learning performance data and utilize such data to guide further instruction. The position requires teachers to utilize research-based and innovative practices to leverage student learning in the areas of core content and 21st-century skills and knowledge and skills from a surface to a deep level of understanding.

Given the high level of expertise of the staff, the involvement level with all stakeholders, and the mass of research related to professional learning, the teacher must be well prepared to engage with stakeholders in an effort to build relationships and enhance the educational experience of adults and children.

Step 2: Filter Candidates Through Screeners

Lead learners need to identify whether educators that are interested in becoming part of their staff have the key belief system necessary to have a long-term likelihood of making a substantial impact on all learners. To do so, a tool is needed that can serve as a preliminary means to screen applicants based on their potential for success within an educational system. This text recommends a short 10-question survey (see Figure 4.7) that applicants can take at the end of their application.

Figure 4.7 Sample Questions to Screen Prospective Teachers

Screener				
Achievement can be changed or enhanced by the actions of the teacher and the student. I see my primary responsibility as substantially changing achievement levels of every student over time.				
Strongly Disagree	Disagree	Neutral	Agree	Strongly Agree
I spend the majority of my time evaluating my efficacy as a teacher on impacting student learning.				

Screener				
Strongly Disagree	Disagree	Neutral	Agree	Strongly Agree
Understanding learning, how people learn, and what principles dictate my actions are more important and interesting to me than discussing curriculum and instruction.				
Strongly Disagree	Disagree	Neutral	Agree	Strongly Agree
I collect feedback from multiple sources to evaluate my own impact on learning and learners.				
Strongly Disagree	Disagree	Neutral	Agree	Strongly Agree
I find that engaging in dialogue with students on where they are going, where they are, and identifying what's next is critical to evaluate their performance and my own and to co-construct next steps with students to move learning forward.				
Strongly Disagree	Disagree	Neutral	Agree	Strongly Agree
I find that teaching students, their families, and the community about learning and learning strategies to promote an understanding of learning is important for student growth in their learning.				
Strongly Disagree	Disagree	Neutral	Agree	Strongly Agree
I think learning requires challenge, and providing students with this understanding is critical to their development.				
Strongly Disagree	Disagree	Neutral	Agree	Strongly Agree
I continually share evidence of my impact with colleagues and seek their input and feedback to learn.				
Strongly Disagree	Disagree	Neutral	Agree	Strongly Agree
I enjoy the struggle of learning and embrace the notion of struggle in my profession as I continually look to improve student learning.				
Strongly Disagree	Disagree	Neutral	Agree	Strongly Agree
I find that collaboration with students and peers requires my active role in establishing mutual respect and trust.				
Strongly Disagree	Disagree	Neutral	Agree	Strongly Agree

Step 3: Engage in Structured Interviews

The next step is for lead learners to find out the likelihood that candidates utilize the beliefs they espouse in practice. The *Structured Interview* is a research-based method of determining a candidate's likelihood for long-term impact on student learning by providing candidates with specific situations in which the beliefs stated in Figure 4.1 need to be expressed. It provides objective information on candidates' relational and tactical acumen and specifically draws out their attitude toward students, focus on substantially enhancing the learning of all students, and likelihood of continuing to improve his or her practice in a collaborative setting. The lead learner uses a "structured interview" to specifically identify certain attributes of candidates. An attribute is the linking of practice and beliefs. Take, for example, questions posed in Figures 4.8 and 4.9.

Only one of these responses links the actions of the teacher to the beliefs listed in Figure 4.1. The response, "Finds ways to understand the student's perspective and identifies ways to provide alternative assessments and different ways to accelerate the student's learning" is directly related to affirming the most appropriate relational and tactical beliefs in specific, and typical, situations that teachers face. Specifically, a positive (+1) response indicates that an educator views himself or herself as a change agent and wants to understand the

---

Figure 4.8   Structured Interview Sample Question—Example #1

We are attempting to find out if a potential candidate possesses the specific beliefs (see below) by answering the following question:

Relational Belief: We are change agents

Tactical Belief: Assessment as feedback regarding their impact

You have a student who is showing mastery on all the major tasks and assessments but does not do the daily assigned work. How would you work with this student?

In terms of responses, we may see three likely answers.

- (+1) Finds ways to understand the student's perspective and identifies ways to provide alternative assessments and different ways to accelerate the student's learning.
- (0) Expects students to complete the assignments or assigns additional work to the student.
- (−1) Provides punitive consequences to the student.

Figure 4.9   Structured Interview Sample Question—Example #2

We are attempting to find out if a potential candidate possesses the specific beliefs (see below) by answering the following question:

Relational Belief: Talk more about learning than teaching

Tactical Belief: Assessment as feedback regarding their impact

What information do you need before developing a lesson plan for your class?

In terms of responses, we may see three likely answers.

- (+1) Student prior knowledge relative to key content learning outcomes and success criteria
- (0) Focused only on key learning outcomes and success criteria
- (−1) Focused on resources, class structure, and standards

learner's perspective and the data to better enhance learning. Second, this educator sees assessment data as feedback to their own instruction and wants to find out better ways to support the learner. Let's look at another example (see Figure 4.9).

Again, only one of the options provides a positive score for the candidate. The positive (+1) score illustrates that a teacher is very concerned with student learning, specifically, student understanding prior to constructing a lesson. As such, this teacher wants to focus his or her time, energy, and effort on learning rather than have focus on teaching (Belief "talk more about learning than teaching"). Yes, lessons need to be constructed and they need to relate to core standards, but we want to know if teachers see students as a critical part of the equation of constructing a lesson. Moreover, we want to see if teachers use assessment data as feedback when designing lesson planning.

Filtering and structured interviews provide leaders with a clear picture of a teacher's belief system and how those beliefs would play out in typical situations in the classroom, department meeting, and staff room. This picture enables leaders to make a decision on who should proceed to the next step in the hiring process.

An entire structured interview process is provided in the activities section in this chapter, as well as an entire hiring guide/plan for schools and districts in the appendix of the book. Moreover, at the end of this chapter, Figures 4.12 and 4.13 provide resources for hiring administrators. A final word about structured interviews is that they should be calibrated with other leaders to make sure there is consistency in scoring.

Step 4: Conduct General Interviews and Demonstrations

The following step provides a larger stakeholder group the opportunity to understand the candidate's acumen related to substantially enhancing students' learning of content, conative, and cognitive knowledge and skills from a surface, to deep, to transfer level. The interview (see Figure 4.10) and demonstration lessons (see Figure 4.11) are myopic in that they focus on the candidate's perspective and knowledge and skills related to their impact on the learning of children.

Lead learners ensure that candidates engage in an interview and demonstration that focuses on tactical skills related to the following key areas:

- **Clarity:** Students need to be absolutely clear on what they are expected to learn, where they are in their learning, and what next steps they need to take to advance their learning. Their understanding and use of content knowledge and skills should transcend any project situation or context.
- **Coherence:** Students need to have a consistent balance of surface, deep, and transfer knowledge and to thoroughly understand and apply content to real-world challenging problems. Each level of content complexity requires different instructional interventions, tasks, and feedback.
- **Capacity:** Students need to be able to talk about their learning, monitor their learning, advocate for next steps in their learning, and be a part of a culture that focuses on and models such efforts.

The process for engaging in this aspect of the process includes a general interview and three brief demonstration activities. General interview questions focus on how teachers use clarity, challenge, and culture when developing and implementing pedagogy, intervening in relation to student feedback (performance and perspective), and collaboration with students and colleagues on improvement in teaching and learning.

Once the interview has concluded, a sequence of demonstration scenarios is provided to the candidate. The first demonstration is preparation—submit a lesson plan that illustrates the teaching of content, conative, and cognitive skills from surface to deep. Second, implement the lesson plan at the initial stage; third, evaluate impact data with a team of teachers.

Figure 4.10   Sample Large Group Interview Questions

1. Introductory Prompt: Please provide us with a brief description of your background and why you are interested in ensuring children in our school learn at high levels.

2. Describe a process of how children learn and how that process influences the way you teach.

3. What appear to be the most important influences in supporting students in learning? How do you ensure students acquire new information and new skills? What appears to be the most important influences in supporting students who have a thorough understanding of the standard or concept you expect students to learn? How do you support students as they move beyond the expectations of the lesson?

4. Tell us about a time when you effectively supported students in your class to learn at high levels. What were the key factors that made that experience so effective?

5. How did you adapt instruction to different individuals? What were key takeaways from this specific situation?

6. What role do you think teachers serve in department and staff meetings?

7. Tell us about a time your contributions had a positive impact on your department and the school.

   What was your primary goal and why?

   How did your colleagues respond?

   Moving forward, how might you build on this?

8. Tell us how you determine your own efficacy of a teacher.

9. Tell us about a time when despite your best efforts a student(s) in the class was/were not meeting your expectations in learning.

   What steps did you take to resolve the problem?

   What was the outcome?

   What could you have done differently?

10. Tell us about a time when a class was not meeting your behavioral expectations.

    What steps did you take to resolve the problem?

    What was the outcome?

    What could you have done differently?

11. Tell us about a time you had difficulty working with a colleague or parent.

    What steps did you take to resolve the problem?

    What was the outcome?

    What could you have done differently?

(Continued)

Figure 4.10 (Continued)

12. Tell us a time when you experienced students who had academically exceeded your expectations *before* you taught a lesson.

    What did you do in response?

    How did you adapt instruction to different individuals?

    What were key takeaways from this specific situation?

13. Discuss your approach to collecting, monitoring, and analyzing assessment data to inform instruction. What experience have you had with involving students in self-assessment?

Figure 4.11 Demonstration Rubric

Lesson Design	Classroom Engagement	Collective Efficacy
❏ Designed to support students in understanding the learning intention and success criteria of the lesson ❏ Designed to provide adequate rigor (surface, deep, and transfer) ❏ Instructional strategies are appropriate to levels of learning and subject matter ❏ Designed to ensure student prior knowledge is identified and acted upon	❏ Connects with students personally and positively ❏ Activates prior knowledge and uses that information to connect students to the learning expectations of the lesson ❏ Uses feedback strategies to improve learning and teaching ❏ Intervenes related to evidence of student performance ❏ Engages students to give and receive feedback from one another ❏ Ensures students know the expectations of the lesson	❏ Analyzes the data to determine efficacy of their teaching practice ❏ Draws inferences that celebrate potential strengths and challenges ❏ Determines next steps to improve learning ❏ Seeks feedback from peers to improve the teaching and learning process ❏ Seeks to involve students in monitoring their individual progress, determining next steps, and giving the teacher feedback on their work
Comments:	Comments:	Comments:

Once all of the information about each candidate has been collected, the hiring committee will provide a recommendation to the leadership team. The steps the committee takes to provide the recommendation include the following:

- **Step 1:** *Reinforce goal*—Remind the hiring committee that the purpose of this work is to find the right person not the best person from the group. As such, there should be no forced ranking, only a determination if the candidate meets the expectations of the position.
- **Step 2:** *Review performance*—Hiring committee discusses the performance relative to the success criteria illustrated on the demonstration rubric.
- **Step 3:** *Potential leverage and support needs*—Hiring committee provides suggested areas of strength that will complement the school or organization as well as potential areas of support.
- **Step 4:** *Recommendation*—Committee makes recommendation to the principal on whether the candidate meets the criteria for hire.

Step 5: Provide Targeted Feedback and Support

Once hired, the wealth of data gathered during the interview process should be used to target feedback and specialize professional development for each individual and the group. The next chapter provides strategies for leaders to engage in capacity building. Leaders should look for themes and patterns with all new hires to better gauge overall professional development for staff. This is what the next chapter is all about.

CONCLUSION

The current chapter argued that the right beliefs and behaviors are essential for hiring and developing educators to make a substantial impact on student learning. The chapter focused specific steps lead learners may take to ensure that the hiring process is focused on identifying and developing employees to substantially enhance student learning in 21st-century learning and includes input from all stakeholders. The next chapter focuses on the lead learners' approach to professional learning.

REFLECTION QUESTIONS

1. How does the following personnel approach differ from your current system-wide practice? What are the key differences? Why?

2. Of the three key elements—beliefs, behaviors, and building capacity—which do you think is most effectively addressed in your current system? What makes you say what? Where do you see the need for major improvements?

3. Which bias do you think is most effectively addressed in your current human resources system? What makes you say what?

4. Which beliefs and behaviors do you think are most effectively explored and addressed in your current human resources system? Where do you see the need for major improvements?

5. Where do you see flexibility in this process?

ACTIVITIES

ACTIVITY 4.1: GAPS AND BRIDGES

On a sheet of paper, create two columns. Label the left column "Current Practice" and the right column "Recommended Practice." Next, compare and contrast current personnel processes with those proposed in this chapter. To assist in this activity, review the sample hiring guide in the Appendix against the references materials in your school or district office. What similarities and difference do you notice? What next steps will you take in light of discrepancies?

ACTIVITY 4.2: ESTABLISHING RELIABILITY

Ask a leader to be filmed as you interview him or her using the structured interview below (Figure 4.12). Next, watch the film with several other administrators and review your scores. Where were you aligned? Where did you find differences? What next steps can you take to develop interrater reliability?

Figure 4.12   Structured Interview for Teachers

Question 1	You have a student who is showing mastery on all core tasks and assessments but does not do the daily assigned work. How would you work with this student?		
Mind frame #1: I am an evaluator of my teaching.	(−1) Provide punitive consequences to the student.	(0) Expect students to complete the assignments or assign additional work to the student.	(+1) Seek to understand the reason(s) the student is not completing the assignments and identify ways to provide alternative assessments and different ways to accelerate the student's learning.
Question 2	You have just reviewed data at the end of a six-week period and students have mixed results regarding their performance. How would you use this data?		
Mind frame #2: I am a change agent.	(−1) Views the data as summative, report the scores, and move on to the next unit.	(0) View the data as feedback for students but don't give students an opportunity to improve *or* don't view the data as related to the teacher's performance	(+1) The entire data are reflective of my (the teacher's) impact, and I would discuss how I would take action to improve student learning.
Question 3	What information do you need before developing a lesson for your class?		
Mind frame #3: I talk more about learning than teaching.	(−1) Focus on resources, class structure, and standards.	(0) Focus only on key learning outcomes and success criteria.	(+1) Student prior knowledge relative to key content learning outcomes and success criteria.

(Continued)

Figure 4.12 (Continued)

Question 4	As students enter the class, you find that the majority of them did not complete the homework from the night before and have remarked to you that they don't understand the material. How would you work with these students?		
Mind frame #4: I see feedback as an assessment of my impact on learning	(−1) Provide punitive consequences to the students.	(0) Expect students to complete homework; don't seek to find out the reasons for the students' decision to not complete the homework.	(+1) Explore reasons why students didn't understand the material and ask for feedback to support them in the future.
Question 5	A small group of students remark to you that they are concerned with the way you have disciplined one of their peers. How would you work with these students?		
Mind frame #5: I engage in dialogue not monologue	(−1) Disregard the students' comments.	0 Let the students speak and then go back to teaching.	(+1) Listen to students' perspective and concerns and provide rationale while staying open to other approaches; stay open to options in the present case or in the future.
Question 6	Some teachers find teaching students to be challenging. Have you ever found teaching challenging? (If yes, proceed to next step in the question.) Please provide an example of a challenging moment during your teaching.		
Mind frame #6: I enjoy challenge	(−1) No, teaching is not a challenging endeavor	(0) Teaching is challenging due to the types of students, fiscal constraints, home life, or administration. Example is focused away from the teacher and his, her, or their teaching.	(+1) Teaching is difficult due to the complexity of perspectives, prior knowledge, and opinions of children, which is also what makes the work exciting. Example is focused on supporting students in an active way.

Question 7	You begin the school year with a group of students who have been known to be challenging to other teachers and administrators. How would you work with these students?		
Mind frame #7: I establish positive relationships in the classroom and staff room	(−1) Articulate punitive expectations to students at the beginning of the classroom	(0) Spend time articulating why they should follow rules	(+1) Establish relationships with students and actively involve them in developing classroom expectations
Question 8	You are planning a beginning of the year meeting with your students' parents to discuss the course you are teaching. How would you work with the parents?		
Mind frame #8: I inform all about the language of learning	(−1) Articulate rules and procedures with no input	(0) Provide tools to support parents at home and articulate learning outcomes for the year	(+1) Listen to parents on their interests and learn about their children; provide tools to support parents at home and articulate learning outcomes for the year
Question 9	You have a student who continues to not meet performance expectations in your classroom. He or she has talked with you about how he or she has continued to try to get better but seems to show no improvement. How would you work with this student?		
Mind frame #9: I see learning as hard work	(−1) Focus on fixed mindsets or student's failures as a negative	(0) Reinforce that student should "try harder"	(+1) Listen to student's strategies they have used so far and work collectively to develop a plan
Question 10	You just entered a meeting with other staff members who are discussing the importance of basic-level knowledge and skills vs. complex-level knowledge and skill. How would you contribute?		

(Continued)

Figure 4.12 (Continued)

Mind frame #10: I collaborate.	(−1) Lack an interest in listening and/or would argue that decisions are based on student characteristics/demographics.	(0) Listen but lack a vague stance on which to support or refute.	(+1) Listen to others' thoughts and ideas; recognize the importance of both/and for basic and complex skills; don't look for student characteristics to make decisions.
Question 11	What draws you toward being a teacher? As such, how would you evaluate your effectiveness as a teacher?		
Mind frame #1: I am an evaluator of my teaching.	(−1) Personal reasons (I like teaching); evaluate performance based on student proficiency.	(0) Help students learn; look at data but don't see this as ongoing.	(+1) Student progress and proficiency in learning core content and affective (or "life") skills; continuously evaluate effectiveness based on student learning.
Question 12	If I were to poll your students right now and ask them how they would describe you as their teacher, what would they say? Why would they say that?		
Mind frame #2: I am a change agent.	(−1) Respect, because of my role as a teacher	(0) Role model, knowledgeable	(+1) Caring, challenging, passionate, and supportive, because I'm constantly seeking to know my students as people and help them develop
Question 13	A fellow teacher comes up to you and is angry that you challenged his or her ideas in front of other faculty. How would you handle that situation?		

Mind frame #3: I talk more about learning than teaching.	(−1) Dismiss remarks.	(0) Listen to their perspective, state rationale for challenging idea; don't see a need to resolve the issue with the other teacher.	(+1) Listen to their perspective and find ways to share positive intent and collectively plan next steps.
Question 14	How do you gain input into your students' performance? What do you do with that data?		
Mind frame #4: I see feedback as an assessment of my impact on learning.	(−1) Focus on student and colleague perception data (other than proficiency and performance data).	(0) Growth and performance data are articulated through multiple assessments; plans are vague.	(+1) Various types of assessments (informal and formal) to determine student progress and proficiency; data are used to inform next steps in instruction with colleagues and students.
Question 15	On a scale of 1–5, with a 1 being the lowest score and 5 being the highest score, how would you rank the importance of listening to others? What are some examples of how you listen to others?		
Mind frame #5: I engage in dialogue not monologue.	(−1) 1–5; examples do not include taking action from listening.	(0) 1–5; listening includes vague examples.	(+1) 5; listening includes examples where collective action was taken.
Question 16	How have you continued to improve as an educator?		
Mind frame #6: I enjoy challenge.	(−1) Don't see this as important; lack details	(0) Only district-required professional development; do not discuss performance data from own classroom.	(+1) Routine professional development in/out of school district to enhance learning; use data from own classroom to drive PD needs.
Question 17	How do you gain insight into how students are feeling in your classroom? What do you do with that information?		

(Continued)

Figure 4.12 (Continued)

Mind frame #7: I establish positive relationships in the classroom and staff room.	(−1) No established strategies are presented; no plan.	(0) General classroom strategies are explained; plan is vague.	(+1) 1:1 strategies to understand student interests and perspectives on a daily basis; information is used to continually build relationships and inform instruction.
Question 18	As you start your next lesson, what do you do to prepare students for learning?		
Mind frame #8: I inform all about the language of learning.	(−1) No clear plan; do not ensure student clarity of expectations	(0) Learning intentions and success criteria; vague plan	(+1) Prior knowledge, learning intentions, and success criteria; articulate a well-thought-out plan
Question 19	What do you expect students will achieve as a result of being under your care for one year? How will you ensure that these expectations happen?		
Mind frame #9: I see learning as hard work.	(−1) Focus on social-emotional development only, excitement, engagement in class.	(0) Focus on content knowledge only; no specific ways of ensuring these expectations are clarified.	(+1) Integrate content and affective growth and proficiency; specific ways to ensure learning in both areas are articulated.
Question 20	You are in the middle of a presentation to students when one student raises her hand and says that she does not understand what you are saying. How would you react to this situation?		
Mind frame #10: I collaborate.	(−1) Ignore	(0) Come back to the students later or stop everyone all together and answer one question.	(+1) Involve other students in the discussion to understand if others are struggling and/or others have ways to support the student; 1:1 strategies may also be used.

Note: The structured interview process and question structure is based on the work of Pete Pillsbury and Target Success. The mind frames are based on John Hattie's *Visible Learning for Teachers* (2012) and are referenced in Figures 4.2 and 4.3.

ACTIVITY 4.3: ADMINISTRATIVE HIRING

Similar to Activity 4.2, to develop a level of reliability in interviewing others, ask a colleague if he or she would be willing to be interviewed using the structured interview below (see Figure 4.13). In addition, request that the interviewee be filmed so that others may use the video to calibrate scoring (Figure 4.14). Next, watch the film with several other administrators and review your scores. Where were you aligned? Where did you find differences? What next steps can you take to develop interrater reliability?

Figure 4.13 Administrative Hiring Brief

Similar to teachers, the efficacy of educational leaders is largely dictated by the set of beliefs and actions they take in the school or district office. *"The more leaders focus their influence, their learning, and their relationships with teachers on the core business of teaching and learning, the greater their likely influence on student outcomes"* (Robinson, Lloyd, & Rowe, 2008, p. 23). Robinson (2011) found that effective leaders establish goals and expectations related to student achievement; resource school strategically; ensure quality teaching, lead teacher learning and development; and ensure an orderly and safe environment. Of all of these actions, leading teacher learning and development had the greatest impact on student learning (Es .84). The idea that educational leaders have such a significant impact on student achievement is largely unrecognized and often goes against the grain of popular thinking on the role and responsibilities of site and district administrators. Typically, an administrator is often viewed as someone who is inspirational, easily accessible, monitors school activities, ensures a high level of autonomy, ensures fair and equitable staffing and scheduling, and buffers staff from external demands.

Administrators who conduct their business by these actions alone have little direct or indirect impact on the achievement of children. School leaders who focus on the achievement of students and work to identify and reproduce strategies that have the greatest impact on learning. Thus, school leaders possess the same beliefs as those described for teachers and utilize, primarily, the actions articulated above.

Figure 4.14 Administrator Structured Interview

Administrator Structured Interview	
Question 1	What is the best way to evaluate your performance as a leader in a school system?

(Continued)

Figure 4.14 (Continued)

Administrator Structured Interview			
Mind frame #1: I am an evaluator of my leadership.	(−1) Visibility, perception of calm/ease in district, affability with others, monitoring of school activities, and execution of basic operations	(0) Level of motivation, level of accessibility, level of autonomy given/provided, buffering staff from external demands	(+1) Student performance, stakeholder feedback related to focus on learning and atmosphere conducive to learning, and coordinated and clear plans and systems related to learning, involvement in professional development, and teaching and learning
Question 2	You have just reviewed overall student performance data at the end of the six-week period and have found that some students showed high growth and reached proficiency and many students showed low growth and did not meet proficiency expectations. How would you use these data with staff?		
Mind frame #2: I am a change agent.	(−1) Data are not necessarily a key factor for staff meetings or discussions.	(0) The data would be used as a reference for administration or other teachers to review; leaders do not see implications of data as their core responsibility, or do not believe it is critical to be involved in processing the data with staff.	(+1) Share data with the staff and discuss ways to understand the data, identify key themes and patterns, and identify next steps to take action in the short term and long term; the focus of the conversation would be on what staff could control.
Question 3	What information do you need before engaging in a staff meeting with your faculty?		

Administrator Structured Interview			
Mind frame #3: I talk more about learning than teaching.	(−1) Logistical needs of staff (or other stakeholders)	(0) Operational progress related to organizational areas (i.e., H.R., finance, facilities, educational services)	(+1) Teacher prior knowledge relative to the strategic plan, student performance data, and teacher professional development needs/interests
Question 4	Several teachers provide you with feedback stating that too many initiatives have been asked of them to engage in and complete this year from you and other administrators. How would you work with teachers on this challenge?		
Mind frame #4: I see feedback as an assessment of my impact on learning.	(−1) Ignore or identify ways to solve the problem without involving staff.	(0) Explore reasons why teachers have this perception and identify potential ways to solve problem (individually, without staff input).	(+1) Explore reasons why teachers have this perception and identify potential ways to solve problem (with staff).
Question 5	A small group of teachers disagrees with the solution that you have proposed for the school. How would you work with these teachers?		
Mind frame #5: I engage in dialogue not monologue.	(−1) Disregard the teachers' comments.	(0) Let the teachers speak and then go back to teaching.	(+1) Listen to teacher perspective and concerns and provide rationale while staying open to other approaches; stay open to options in the present case or in the future.
Question 6	Some leaders find leading teachers to be challenging. Have you ever found leadership of people to be challenging? (If yes, proceed to the next question.) Please provide an example of a challenging moment during your leadership.		

(Continued)

Figure 4.14   (Continued)

Administrator Structured Interview			
Mind frame #6: I enjoy challenge.	(−1) No, leading is not a challenging endeavor.	(0) Leading is challenging due to the types of employees, students, fiscal constraints, home life, or administration. Example is focused on outside influences or the view that people can't change (and the leader must work around them).	(+1) Leading is difficult due to the complexity of perspectives, prior knowledge, and opinions of stakeholders, which is also what makes the work exciting. Example is focused on supporting stakeholders in an active way.
Question 7	You begin the school year with a group of teachers that have been known to be challenging to other teachers and administrators on reviewing student performance data and determining solutions that are within the control of the staff. How would you work with these teachers?		
Mind frame #7: I establish positive relationships in the classroom and staff room.	(−1) Articulate punitive expectations to teachers at the beginning of the school year (cite the contract) or work around the staff (disengage or ignore resistant staff).	(0) Spend time articulating why they should follow rules.	(+1) Establish relationships with teachers and actively involve entire staff in developing solutions.
Question 8	You are planning a beginning of the year meeting with parents to discuss the work of your school/district. How would you work with your parents?		
Mind frame #8: I inform all about the language of learning.	(−1) Articulate rules and procedures with no input.	(0) Provide tools to support parents at home and articulate goals for the year.	(+1) Listen to parents on their interests and learn about their children; provide tools to support parents at home and articulate goals for the year.

Administrator Structured Interview			
Question 9	You have several teachers that continue to not meet performance expectations despite the best efforts of you and your team. They have talked with you about how they have continued to try to get better but seem to show no improvement. How would you work with these teachers?		
Mind frame #9: I see learning as hard work.	(−1) Focus on fixed mindsets or teacher failures as a negative; fire the teachers.	(0) Reinforce that teachers should "try harder."	(+1) Listen to teachers' strategies they have used so far and work collectively to develop a plan.
Question 10	You just entered a meeting with other staff members who are discussing the importance of basic-level knowledge and skills vs. complex-level knowledge and skill. How would you contribute?		
Mind frame #10: I collaborate.	(−1) Lack an interest in listening and/or argue that decisions are based on student characteristics/ demographics	(0) Listen but lack a vague stance on which to support or refute	(+1) Listen to others' thoughts and ideas; recognize the importance of both/ and for basic and complex skills; don't look for student characteristics to make decisions
Question 11	What draws you toward being a leader? As such, how would you evaluate your effectiveness as a leader?		
Mind frame #1: I am an evaluator of my leadership.	(−1) Personal reasons (I like leading/being in charge); evaluate performance based on student proficiency and teacher view of their leadership.	(0) Helping student and teachers learn; look at data but don't see this as ongoing.	(+1) Student progress and proficiency in learning core content and affective (or "life") skills; building capacity of teachers and other stakeholders. Continuously evaluate effectiveness based on student learning.

(Continued)

Figure 4.14   (Continued)

Administrator Structured Interview			
Question 12	If I were to poll your teachers right now and ask them how they would you describe you as their leader, what would they say? Why would they say that? What about students in your school/district?		
Mind frame #2: I am a change agent.	(−1) Respect, because of my role as a leader.	(0) Role model, knowledgeable; dissimilar feedback from stakeholders	(+1) Caring, challenging, passionate, and supportive. Because I'm constantly seeking to know my teachers as people and help them develop. Similar feedback from all stakeholders.
Question 13	A teacher comes up to you and is angry that you challenged his or her ideas in front of other faculty. How would you handle that situation?		
Mind frame #3: I talk more about learning than teaching.	(−1) Dismiss remarks.	(0) Listen to perspective and do nothing or capitulate without collectively understanding and discussing next steps.	(+1) Listen to perspective and find ways to share positive intent and collectively plan next steps.
Question 14	How do you gain input into your students' performance? What do you do with that data?		
Mind frame #4: I see feedback as an assessment of my impact on learning.	(−1) Focus on student and colleague perception data (other than proficiency and performance data)	(0) Growth and performance data are articulated through multiple assessments; plans are vague	(+1) Various types of assessments (informal and formal) to determine student progress and proficiency; data are used to inform next steps in the leader's actions

Administrator Structured Interview			
Question 15	On a scale of 1–5, with a 1 being the lowest score and 5 being the highest score, how would you rank the importance of listening to others? What are some examples of how you listen to others?		
Mind frame #5: I engage in dialogue not monologue.	(–1) 1–5; examples do not include taking action from listening.	(0) 1–5; listening includes vague examples.	(+1) 5; listening includes examples where collective action was taken.
Question 16	How have you continued to improve as an educational leader?		
Mind frame #6: I enjoy challenge.	(–1) Don't see this as important; lacks detail.	(0) Only district-required professional development; do not discuss performance data from school or school system.	(+1) Routine professional development in/ out of school district to enhance learning; use data from school or school system to drive PD needs.
Question 17	How do you gain insight into how teachers are feeling in your school/system? What do you do with that information?		
Mind frame #7: I establish positive relationships in the classroom and staff room.	(–1) No established strategies are presented; no plan.	(0) General strategies for outreach are explained; plan is vague.	(+1) Strategies to understand teacher interests and perspectives are explained in detail; information is used to continually build relationships and inform leadership.
Question 18	As you start your next meeting, what do you do to prepare the group/team for learning?		
Mind frame #8: I inform all about the language of learning.	(–1) No clear plan; doesn't ensure staff clarity of expectations	(0) Learning intentions and success criteria; vague plan	(+1) Prior knowledge, learning intentions, success criteria; articulate a well-thought-out plan

(Continued)

Figure 4.14 (Continued)

Administrator Structured Interview			
Question 19	What do you expect teachers will achieve as a result of being under your care for one year? How will you ensure that these expectations occur?		
Mind frame #9: I see learning as hard work.	(−1) Focus only on district-approved performance goals; lack discussion on progress and proficiency; lack discussion on supporting teachers to improve in their performance.	(0) Integrate school goals with teacher-selected goals; no specified ways to ensure teachers are evaluating and discussing their performance and taking actions to continually improve are discussed.	(+1) Integrate school goals with teacher-selected goals; specify ways to ensure teachers are evaluating and discussing their performance and taking actions to continually improve.
Question 20	You are in the middle of a presentation to teachers when one teacher raises her hand and says that she does not understand what you are saying. How would you react to this situation?		
Mind frame #10: I collaborate.	(−1) Ignore.	(0) Come back to the teacher later or stop everyone all together and answer one question.	(+1) Involve other teachers in the discussion to understand if others are struggling and/or others have ways to support the teacher; 1:1 strategies may also be used.

NEXT STEPS

1. Create and adopt a hiring guide that is aligned to the school/system strategic plan.

2. Begin practicing with interviewing tools for hiring to ensure familiarity and reliability.

3. Develop an analysis of strengths and weaknesses of new hires. Consider strategies in the next chapter to support staff development over time.

5

Capacity

Community Learning

Culture is comprised of deeply embedded processes or patterns of working together that employees instinctively follow—and that these processes are responses to the problems that a group has repeatedly and successfully confronted in its path—then attempts to change culture or process by directly attacking culture are unlikely to result in significant changes.

—Christensen (1999)

The central issue is never strategy or structure, it is always about changing the behavior of people.

—Kotter & Cohen (2002)

I live 20 miles from the epicenter of innovation, Silicon Valley. When one thinks of Silicon Valley, they are likely to imagine ping-pong tables, free food, and lively collaborative working spaces. We are often fed books, articles, and tweets that extol such artifacts as the ideals of working culture yielding the products and services required of today and a healthy and positive culture for employees. As an educator, I can admit that such a culture sounds impressive and I have an impulse every day to fly out to a school and bear witness to new learning spaces, collaborative "hubs" for teachers to work in, and new approaches to professional development that provide educators with complete autonomy to engage in teaching and learning. Leaders, of course, will take note that these organizations often possess effective norms or agreements of how to operate, a strong vision, and a philosophy that underpins excellence today and in the future. However, these artifacts tell us nothing about the essence of the culture of the organization.

What tells us about the essence of the organization's culture is the tasks organizations face and how they face them. Culture is all about how the collective answers the question *how do the people in an organization solve the tasks of the organization?* And what tasks does the organization work to solve? Put differently, culture is the collective response to recurring tasks that the organization faces. So far in this book, we have seen that lead learners establish a clear plan of action, create a system to enable educators to review and respond to student learning, and select educators who are willing and able to support all students in their learning. Now the book turns to engaging all educators in building their capacity through continuous improvement as a means to solve the recurring task of substantially enhancing learning.

Building Capacity Through Continuous Improvement

- Lead learners focus squarely on creating standardized criteria for learning while embracing customizable approaches to how educators learn.
- Lead learners are not interested in fidelity to a certain approach to learning (or teaching) but rather that certain approaches to learning (or teaching) are anchored in principles of cognitive science.
- Correspondingly, lead learners are not interested in fidelity to a certain way for adults to learn but that their learning is anchored in quality principles of improvement science.
- As such, lead learners scale success criteria for learning across the system and leave pathways or approaches to learning for teachers, administrators, and schools to decide.
- They do this by articulating standardized success criteria and offering organizational routines that have a high probability of improving adult learning.

Standardized Success Criteria

Lead learners deploy the following four key criteria for professional learning (or continuous improvement) across the educational system:

Stay small, stay focused—All professional learning is centered on strategies informed by students' progress and proficiency data.

Short term—All professional learning is implemented in short cycles of inquiry through deliberate practice and tangible, reachable outcomes.

Shared learning—Learning across the system and external research and practice are shared across the system to curate learning and support and challenge current thinking and practice.

Self-directed—All professional learning is self-selected (within the parameters of the goals of the organization) by professionals driven by the needs of learners.

Customizable Organizational Routines for Learning

Lead learners offer a variety of organizational routines that educators may use to codify the standardized success criteria, including

- critical friends teams (CFTs),
- student involvement in the CFT process,
- learning rounds,
- learning convening (meeting reboot), and
- professional learning events.

VOICES FROM THE FIELD

Joanna Mitchell, Principal

North Tahoe High School, Tahoe Truckee Unified School District

Truckee, California

Educational change is often a long process that requires effective leadership to facilitate a sound continuous improvement process. This process requires a "both/and" mindset. Teams are a key driver to carry out this mindset in an effort to improve learning for all. Effective leaders help their team define their overarching goals and the rationale behind those goals; they have the organization to create and implement action plans and the flexibility to change the plan when necessary; and they have the patience and resolution necessary to hold the goal up to their team and refocus them over and over again.

Before any team can be formed, a common goal must be defined. In education, this means identifying team core beliefs, like "every student can

(Continued)

(Continued)

and wants to learn and succeed." Identifying these core beliefs helps a team determine their goals or "where we are going." Once the goal is determined, a detailed and honest needs assessment must take place. This is a very rational, data-driven process in which a team must identify their strengths and challenges. This must be done openly, without blame, and in a fashion that models the growth mindset we want to foster in our students. This helps a team define "where we are at now." Finally, the team must decide what steps must be taken to get from "where we are at now" to "where we are going." This is the foundation of a sound continuous improvement process. It is a whole brain approach because it intertwines the creative process of establishing a vision and the concrete process of analyzing data and action planning. Revisiting these goals and action plan, reporting on progress each year, and setting new targets is an essential part of framing the work that we do as educators. Without this process of getting everyone on the same page, any educational reform or initiative lacks a sense of "why we are doing this."

Critical Friends Teams

One organizational routine is to have educators work in teams to give and receive feedback on their impact in the classroom. A critical friends team (CFT) is a team of educators whose core purpose is to understand and act upon teachers' impact on student learning. By establishing a clear sense of progress and proficiency, teams may come together to review evidence, develop potential diagnoses, develop potential interventions, and evaluate their decisions over time.

To engage in this work, teams need to have clear ways of engaging in dialogue that ensure critical feedback is provided while also maintaining trust and respect. To do this, CFTs need to spend time structuring dialogue to ensure everyone is "hard on content" and "soft on people." One way to do this is to establish agreements (or norms) and protocols (structured ways to engage in dialogue). Figure 5.1 illustrates several agreements and protocols that could be used by a CFT. This text leans on the work of Argyris, Putnam, and McLain Smith (1985) and Roger Schwarz (2016), who articulated the importance of specific agreements that were shown to develop mutual learning for all team members (including leaders of teams). These agreements and protocols are based on the following key assumptions: (1) I have information and so do other people, (2) people may disagree with me and still have pure motives, (3) I may be contributing to the problem, (4) each of us sees things others don't, and (5) differences are opportunities for learning. All protocols referenced in the book can be found in the Appendix.

Figure 5.1   Agreements and Protocols for CFTs

Agreement	Description	Protocols
Test assumptions and inferences	Team members verify assumptions and check inferences against facts during discussions to inform decisions and ensure a trusting culture.	• What?, So What?, Now What? • Consultancy Dilemma
Share all relevant information	Team members share information and perspectives with each other before making a choice.	• Leadership Dilemma • SWOT Analysis • Affinity Mapping • Chalk Talk
Use specific examples and agree on what important words means	Team members ensure that everyone is clear on what is being discussed and acted upon.	• Metaphor • Mind Map • Nominal Group Technique • Pareto Chart • Why Cycle • Tree Diagram • Final Word
Explain your reasoning and intent	Team members articulate the reasons and motives behind their ideas.	• Scenario Building • Issaquah Protocol • Final Word
Focus on interests, not positions	Team members ensure that members' needs, cares, and values are at the center of decision-making and *not* a specific solution.	• Snow Card • Constructivist Listening • T-Chart • Criteria Development
Combine advocacy and inquiry	Team members apply the inquiry method with fellow team members to tease out the thinking and rationale behind the ideas of others. This requires all participants to share and test their views in a safe and supportive space.	• Critical Friends • Constructivist Tuning • Feedback Carousel
Jointly design steps and ways to test disagreement	Team members explore the similarities and differences between various opinions and find common ground.	• Gap Analysis • Cost Iceberg • Contingency Analysis

(Continued)

Figure 5.1 (Continued)

Agreement	Description	Protocols
Discuss undiscussable issues	Team members ensure that members explore challenges that hinder the team's work.	• Personal Power Grid • Boundary Setting Mission Management • Force Field Analysis • Zones of Comfort, Risk, and Danger • Positive Context
Use a decision-making rule that generates commitment needed	Team members are absolutely clear on the team protocol for making a decision and where the boundaries of their decision resides.	• Participative Management Tree • Trade-Off Analysis • Stakeholder Analysis • Future Protocol

Source: Adapted from Arygris and Schon, as cited in McDowell (2017).

Typically, CFTs follow a process for inspecting their impact on learning, identifying and activating next steps to improve learning, and evaluating and reflecting on their impact. Figure 5.2 illustrates a deliberate and replicable problem-solving process that critical friends teams can use to improve learning.

Figure 5.2 Critical Friends Teams Problem-Solving Process

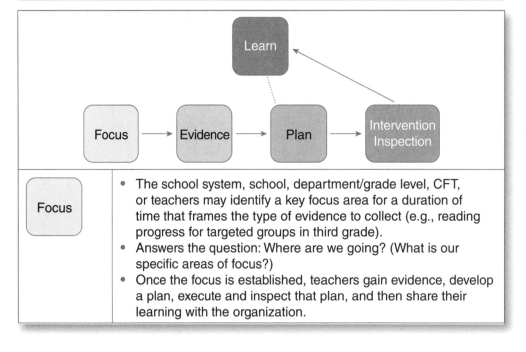

Focus	• The school system, school, department/grade level, CFT, or teachers may identify a key focus area for a duration of time that frames the type of evidence to collect (e.g., reading progress for targeted groups in third grade). • Answers the question: Where are we going? (What is our specific areas of focus?) • Once the focus is established, teachers gain evidence, develop a plan, execute and inspect that plan, and then share their learning with the organization.

Evidence	• All actions of CFTs begin with evidence of student learning. • Individual teachers or CFTs collect student progress and proficiency data (as well as any other data of interest related to learning engagement, school climate, etc.). • Answers the question: Where are we now? (What evidence do I have of student learning?)

Plan	• Teachers and/or CFTs identify a specific goal for student learning.
	• During the planning phase teams may need to (learn) gain more knowledge and skill.
	• The goal that is created is
	   ○ specific to a target group of students (fewer than 20 students),
	   ○ attainable within 3–6 weeks, and
	   ○ measurable within 3–6 weeks.
	• The actions identified by teachers are evaluated by the systems instructional model.
	• The team identifies what they need to learn and how to gain that knowledge or skill.
	• Answers the questions: What's next? (Do I need to build more knowledge and skill? Can we make a meaningful change in a short amount of time? What steps will we take?)

Learn	• Teachers and/or CFTs engage in different professional learning to receive and provide content to move their learning forward (e.g., learning rounds, a learning convening, professional learning events). • Answers the questions: What do we need to learn to develop and execute a plan of action? What did we learn from our implementation of the plan? • Share key learning from the CFT problem-solving process.
Intervention Inspection	• Teachers and the CFT engage in actions (i.e., interventions) and determine if the interventions are making an impact. • Teachers and the CFT continually inspect performance. • Teachers and the CFT contribute their learning to staff and the system. • Teachers and the CFT may re-engage in a new plan of action. • Answers the question: Where are we now? (What happened via the intervention?)

Note: Other processes are found in the Activities section at the end of this chapter.

Student Involvement in the CFT Process

The CFT process may well be enhanced when teachers and *students* work together to evaluate their impact on learning and respond in a manner that ensures a greater level of learning and ownership of learning. As discussed in the introduction, students need to be aware of their own learning, which includes their understanding of the outcomes they are to learn, their current knowledge and skill level relative to those outcomes, and the discrepancy between their current knowledge and skill and summative outcomes. By possessing this understanding, students can take action on the steps necessary to move toward bridging the gap between outcomes and current understanding, and identifying learning strategies they may employ as well as feedback they may provide to the teacher.

Overall, having students discuss their goals, current status, and co-creating next steps would develop a greater sense of building their confidence and advocating for their learning needs as

Figure 5.3   Alignment of CFTs for Students and Teachers

CFT Elements	Student Led	Teacher Led
Focus	Students are focused on answering the questions: Where am I going? Where are you going?	Teachers are focused on answering the questions: Where are we (i.e., teachers, class, school) going? (What is our specific areas of focus?)
Evidence	Students are searching for evidence to answer the questions: Where am I in my learning? Where do you I see myself in building surface, deep, and transfer understanding?	Teachers are focused on answering the questions: Where are we now? (What evidence do I have of student learning?)
Plan	Students are answering the questions: What's next? What's my plan of action to improve?	Teachers are focused on answering the questions: What's next? (Do I need to I need to build more knowledge and skill? Can we make a meaningful change in a short amount of time? What steps will we take?)
Learn	Students are answering the question: What do I see as next steps to enhance my learning?	Teachers are focused on answering the questions: What do we need to learn to develop and execute a plan of action? What did we learn from our implementation of the plan?
Intervention Inspection	Students are answering the questions: What progress am I making? How do I improve my learning and that of others? What have I learned from this process?	Teachers are focused on answering the question: Where are we now? (What happened via the intervention?)

well as giving teachers a wealth of information related to next steps. Furthermore, when teachers are working with students and providing them with feedback, learners start to develop a better sense of how to give each other feedback. Knowing that peer feedback is of high value to learners and most of it is wrong (Nuthall, 2007), this practice may enhance their assessment capabilities and improve the accuracy of feedback. Moreover, when teachers begin seeing the successes and challenges of learners through these CFT meetings, they are able to more effectively intervene.

Learning Rounds

Rather than instructional rounds, which focus on the relationship between the teacher, the student, and the content as it pertains to the task to demonstrate learning (see Figure 5.4; City, Elmore, Fiarman, & Teitel, 2009), lead learners would use an organization routine focused on the "learning core" (see Figure 5.5), which centers on two key areas:

- Process for Learning—Students understand their performance and next steps relative to a learning goal (i.e., orientation to learning), a belief in themselves to grow as a learner and a preparedness to take next steps to improve (i.e., activation), an ability to give and receive feedback (i.e., collaboration), and a strong connection with adults in the room (i.e., relationships with adults).
- Progress of Learning—Students and teachers working together to progress toward core learning intentions and success criteria at each level of complexity (surface, deep, and transfer).

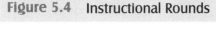

Figure 5.4   Instructional Rounds

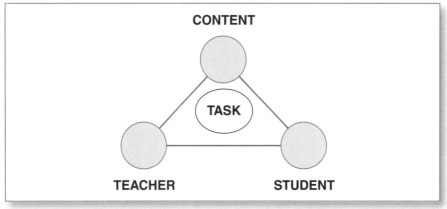

Figure 5.5   Learning Rounds

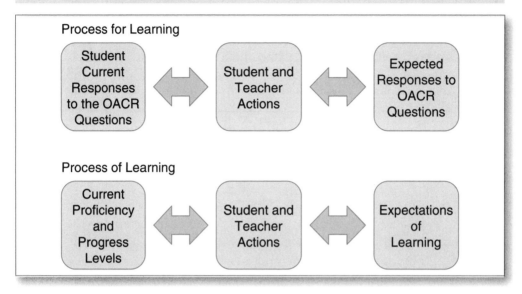

Learning rounds focus on similar questions as those in the CFT process.

Figure 5.6 illustrates the key similarities and differences in instructional vs. learning rounds. Instructional rounds is a useful approach but it focuses on the wrong unit of analysis in name and function as the

Figure 5.6   Instructional vs. Learning Rounds

Elements	Instructional Rounds	Learning Rounds
Focus of the *problem of practice*	• The problem of practice is an instructional problem that the host team wants to solve in order to improve student learning.	• The problem of practice is a learning problem that the host team wants to understand and reconcile by identifying student and teacher actions that may be an appropriate solution to move learning forward in both process for learning and progress of learning.
Focus of the *observation of practice*	• Observers learn to take descriptive notes and pay attention to students and the tasks they are doing—not just what students are being *asked* to do, but what they are *actually* doing.	• Observers take descriptive notes and pay attention to: ○ what students understand (in terms of academic content knowledge and skills) relative to what they are doing,

Elements	Instructional Rounds	Learning Rounds
		○ how they perform relative to learning intentions and success criteria, and students' level of understanding of their own performance ○ Students' beliefs in their ability to improve ○ Students' beliefs in their relationship with adults and other students ○ Students strategies in moving learning forward with others
Focus of the *observational debrief*	• Observers describe what they saw, identify patterns and themes, and develop a hypothesis of the resulting impact on student learning if everything remains the same.	• Observers describe what students thought about relative to their learning and their understanding of how they are learning (e.g., of questions: Where are you going? Where are you now? And what's next?), developed inferences related to student learning, and suggested next steps to improve learning.
Focus on the *next level of work*	• Collectively, the next level of work is created, which may include ○ share district-level theory of action; ○ share district context, including resources, professional development, and current initiatives; ○ brainstorm suggestions for school level and for district level; and ○ tie suggestions to the district's (and school's) theory of action.	• Develop specific next steps for the classroom, CFT, school site, and system. • Articulate actions (i.e., "In light of this data, what are we going to do?") vs. inactions (i.e., "What are we not going to do or stop doing?")

first two steps are drastically different in focus of the problem and data collection. The last two steps are similar in process; however, the results will more than likely be different given the problems to solve and the data collected. Notice the key elements are the same in both models:

- Problem of practice
- Observation of practice
- Observational debrief
- Next level of work

In the activities section of this chapter, two activities are offered (Activities 5.3 and 5.5) that support educators in engaging in this process. Several alternative protocols and resources educators (and learners) may use in engaging in the learning rounds process are presented in the Appendix.

Instructional rounds are an effective strategy, and this text is not denouncing such a practice. This text suggests that learning rounds shifts to learning as the unit of analysis—learning and learners. In many ways, both of these practices could be used in a system. Learning rounds would be an initial step that may be followed by a focus on changing a particular instructional problem of practice, which requires observations of a teacher's skill. Following such work, a learning round would be beneficial to gain evidence of impact.

Learning Convening (Meeting Reboot)

Leaders are frequently faced with facilitating staff meetings with a desire to satisfy everyone's perceived needs, but often they leave the majority of employees confused and lacking substance to the myriad of questions they have. One way for leaders to structure staff meetings is to organize meetings based on the level of question that is typically faced when focused on improvement.

Figure 5.7   Four Types of Meetings

Purpose	• Purpose meetings answer the following questions: *How do we define what is right? Is this the right thing to talk about?* • Purpose meetings are vision-driven conversations that are often divergent, requiring multiple perspectives. Debate should be structured accordingly. • Purpose meetings typically last two hours. They run based on established norms and protocols for conflict, and they are driven by learning data. • Purpose meetings help frame the focus for CFTs. • These are typically done once or twice a year.

Strategic	• Strategic meetings answer the question: *Is what we are doing right?* (Strategy) • Strategy-driven meetings are one hour. They are often showcases for CFTs to discuss their rationale for selecting particular strategies to enhance student learning.
Procedure	• Procedure meetings answer the question: *How do I do this?* (Procedure) • Procedure driven meetings are 30- to 45-minute input sessions that provide targeted instruction on how to implement a particular strategy. Procedure meetings are often structured professional development opportunities developed based on CFT needs. Organizations may have long-day PD events (see next section) that are also associated with the "how to" of teaching and learning.
Logistics	• Logistics meetings answer the question: *What are the specific logistical details we need to take care of today?* • Logistical meetings are 5–10 minutes and limit dialogue and provide specific information regarding topics not related to learning. • Logistical meetings are best conducted by previewing a memo before the meeting and staff stand for the meeting.

When leaders lead these meetings, they should consider the yearly flow: purpose⟶followed by strategic⟶followed by procedural meetings. Leaders should constantly summarize the key learning from CFT teams and use that analysis to determine the greatest leverage for meeting with staff. Figure 5.8 provides an

Figure 5.8 Outlining Professional Learning

Meeting Type	Sample Protocols	Sample Routines	Examples
Purpose	• Stakeholder Analysis • Future Protocol • Boundary Setting • Mission Management	• CFT	*School site has CFTs that come together at the beginning of the second semester to review their core purpose as a team.*
Strategic	• Trade-Off Analysis • Affinity Mapping • Chalk Talk • Let It Go	• CFT	*School sites request that CFTs begin looking at potential strategies that will substantially improve learning.*

(Continued)

Figure 5.8 (Continued)

Meeting Type	Sample Protocols	Sample Routines	Examples
Procedure	• Constructivist Tuning Protocol • Critical Friends • Consultancy Dilemma • Feedback Carousel	• Learning rounds • Professional learning events • CFT	*CFTs meet monthly to develop and refine their skills through specific learning opportunities.*
Logistics	• Constructivist Listening	• CFT	*Team members take a brief period of time before or after meetings to engage in logistical information that impacts their lives and that of their students.*

example of how leaders can outline professional learning for their teams. All of the sample protocols listed in Figure 5.8 can be found in the Appendix.

Professional Learning Events

As staff are using evidence to drive instruction and develop and execute plans of actions, they will inevitably need new knowledge and skills to move their learning and that of their students forward. This is *exactly* what professional learning should be about—just-in-time learning directly related to the needs of the professionals in the field. Stated differently, professional learning events should be structured to alleviate the "gaps" educators have in their learning. In fact, it appears, when professional development is provided and a gap in knowledge is not identified, professional development doesn't improve learning. Robinson (2011) argued,

> They [teachers] may also believe that they are already doing most or all of what is being proposed. This is a common reaction to professional development that does not provide teachers with sufficient opportunities to study the difference between their current practice and the alternative that is being proposed by the professional development provider.

VOICES FROM THE FIELD

Riley Johnson, Principal

Napa New Tech High School

Napa, California

Being a leader at a school that has defined innovation and school reform for the last 20 years can be challenging all by itself. Pushing both student and adult learning to be relevant in the 21st century can be exhaustive and time-consuming. Through my leadership journey, I have found it necessary to ensure that the collective practices of my staff focus on making sure that students are gaining the key academic competencies and knowledge necessary to be able to apply it to authentic 21st-century contexts. This requires clarity, cohesion, and capacity of my team.

I have been able to keep our focus on creating high-quality project-based learning experiences, promoting a truly holistic student-centered environment, and maintaining high academic performance by establishing clarity, cohesion, and capacity. To allow opportunities for this growth in practice, I knew we needed to revisit our strategic plan to adult learning. What we found was that we had ample time available to us within our school day. Our staff agreed to modify our schedule to support an embedded professional learning community (PLC) period in addition to their independent or collaborative prep periods. This approach has allowed our staff to focus on targeted scaffolds for 21st-century skills, create cohesion around project planning and implementation, and use data and looking at student work protocols to refine our practices.

In terms of delivery, we are all conditioned to want PD that is clear and concise and we want inspirational TED Talk–like experiences that provide an emotional stroking and a passive requirement on our behalf. And, I admit, PD can be like seeing a great movie and having a great dinner. And this should be a part of the experience. However, conflict of ideas is essential. We need to debate ideas, not people. As Hargreaves, Boyle, and Harris state (2014, p. 168), "disagreement is the lifeblood of creativity," and as such we should see conference rooms filled with creativity through dialogue and debate.

This is easier said than done. As Brookfield (1986) argues,

But teaching involves pressing alternatives, questioning givens, and scrutinizing the self. The outcome of these activities may be a more satisfactory level of self-insight, but these experiences may induce pain and feelings of insecurity. As teachers, we are charged with not always accepting definitions of felt needs as our operating educational criteria. We are also charged with the imperative of assisting adults to contempt alternatives, to come to see the worlds as malleable, to be critically reflective, and to perceive themselves as proactive beings. (p. 125)

So, how do we construct professional learning in a way that tests prior knowledge, evokes conflict, and enables teams to move forward in their plan of action to improve learning?

Figure 5.9 provides criteria to consider when organizing professional learning.

Figure 5.9 Professional Learning Criteria

COHERENCE	• Align professional learning to the focus of the organization— progress and proficiency of student learning in core academic areas and 21st-century skills. • Align professional learning to the specific action plans of the critical friends teams (or other team structures).
ORIENTATION	• Professional learning requires a pre-assessment of knowledge and skills of staff. (What do they know?) • Professional learning requires that educators identify where they need to go. (What do they need to know?) • Throughout the professional learning events, teachers should evaluate their understanding on session outcomes.
INTERLEAVE	• Professional learning should provide opportunities at surface, deep, and transfer levels of understanding. • Professional learning should ensure that teachers are exposed to more than one level of complexity during an experience.
DIALOGUE	• Teachers need to wrestle with ideas and practices with each other to grow and learn. Professional learning should provide opportunities for teachers to engage with each other.

CONCLUSION

The greatest lever of change is in building capacity of the educators in your care. The means to engage in this process requires significant and substantial involvement of the leader to model and structure effective practice and to be fully present in all professional development. Leaders must model those practices that bring together the actions that are esteemed in both 20th-century and 21st-century environments and bring together both transformational and instructional practices to ensure learning for all. That is precisely the focus of the next chapter.

REFLECTION QUESTIONS

1. Identify the key quality criteria of professional development/ learning for your own organization. How do your quality criteria differ from those proposed in this text?

2. Of the various capacity-building approaches, which does your system execute effectively now? What areas are absent or subpar? What next steps do you need to take to build your own capacity in leading these types of engagements?

3. How do the following ideas support community learning in your environment?

4. Which success criteria are your teams meeting now? What's absent?

5. What do your staff meetings look like relative to the meeting structures presented in this chapter? How would you improve your staff meetings?

ACTIVITIES

ACTIVITY 5.1: IMPROVEMENT SPRINTS

The following activity is adapted from the Agile Schools Improvement Sprints model. The idea fits for a small group of educators to engage in a problem-solving process that relies on lead learner knowledge and skills. To begin, teams should work together to review the purpose of CFTs, review progress and proficiency data, and then use one of the protocols in the Appendix to determine potential strategies to improve learning. Next, the team should set a 1- to 4-week timeline to implement a new strategy, determine efficacy, and then review successes, challenges, and determine next steps. The team should focus on rapid prototyping and adjusting actions based on just-in-time feedback.

Figure 5.10 Agile Schools Learning Sprints

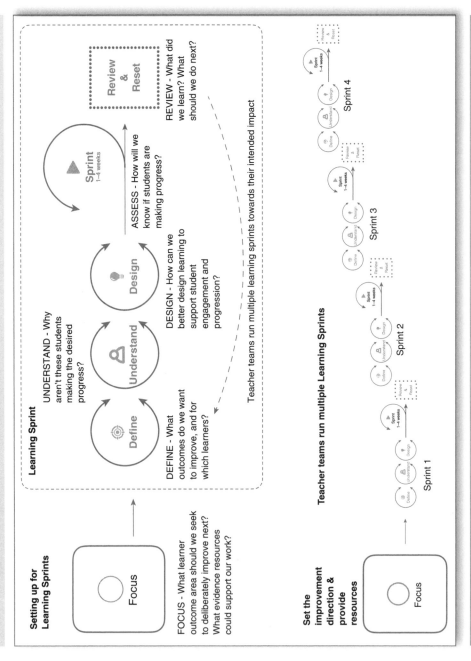

Source: Agile Schools Pty Ltd, n.d.

ACTIVITY 5.2: LEADING THE LEARNING

You are tasked with leading a professional learning event for your staff. The staff has identified a need for supporting students in understanding the relationship between progress and proficiency. Based on the criteria for effective professional learning (see Figure 5.9), the progress and proficiency chart (see below), and the example from one of your teachers, how would you lead this event?

Figure 5.11   Progress and Proficiency Matrix

PROFICIENCY

Transfer Deep   C   A

Surface W/Support   D   B

0–.39   .40+

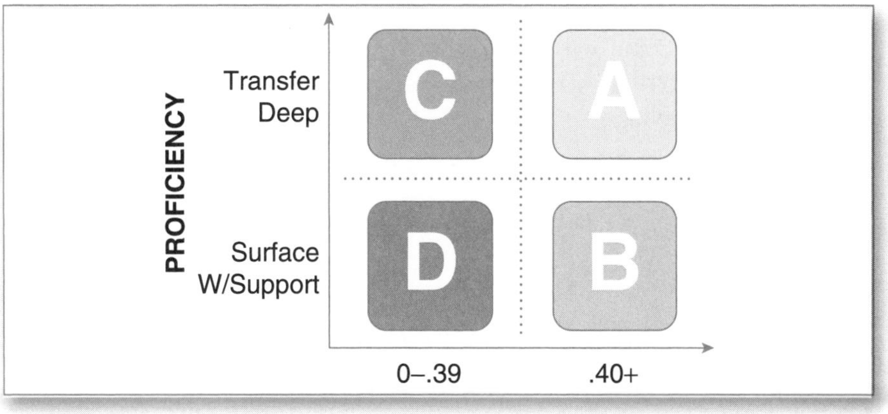

Figure 5.12   Student-Developed Progress and Proficiency Matrix

Source: Gomez, 2017.

ACTIVITY 5.3: LEARNING ROUNDS

The following activity requires leaders (or leadership teams) to consider what they will "look for" and what feedback they will prepare for teachers during a learning rounds session.

Before engaging in a learning rounds process, several teachers submit to you (and the team) a set of images from their classrooms. They tell you that these are artifacts that they have been using to support students in answering the following questions: *Where am I going in my learning?*, *Where am I now?*, *What's next?*, and *How do I improve my learning and that of others?*

After reviewing the following images, develop a series of questions that you have and steps you will take to answer those questions when observing each class. Next, engage in Activity 5.4.

Figure 5.13   Learning Disposition Dichotomy Shift Chart

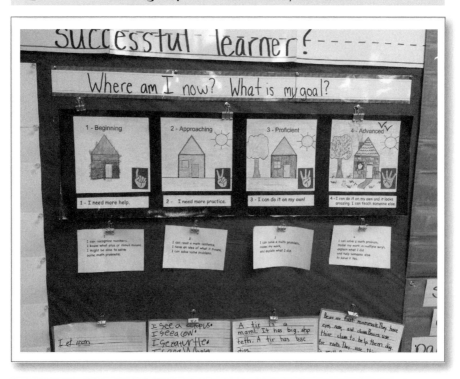

Source: Rolle, 2015.

Figure 5.14   Learning Zones Chart

ACTIVITY 5.4: LEARNING ROUNDS ACTIVITY ROUND II

LEARNING ROUNDS

Guidelines

1. Speak to learners; listen to learners.

2. Don't look at the adults (other than saying hello and goodbye).

3. Provide your notes to the adults in the classroom (with no judgments).

4. Focus on the problems of practice that are identified by the school, class-room teacher, or learners.

Process

1. Divide the questions amongst a group.

    • The questions are based on orientation (a learner's ability to under-stand their performance and next steps relative to a goal), activa-tion (a learner's belief in themselves to grow as a learner and a learner's actions in taking next steps), and collaboration (a learner's ability to give and receive feedback), and relationships (a learner's perspective of the relationship with adults in the room).

2. When you go into a classroom write down only observations—what did you see or hear?

3. After visiting several classrooms, find a place to meet together to discuss the observations, identify inferences, and determine next steps.

4. Elect someone to jot down notes in the following table.

5. Begin with writing down the observations (What?).

6. Next, write down any inferences (So What?).

7. Finally, write down potential suggested next steps (Now What?). Only provide next steps for those who were being observed if they are in the room and are actively participating. If they are not in the room, next steps should be directed toward those who were observing (i.e., What are our next steps?).

Table

	What?	So What?	Now What?
Orientation			
Activation			
Collaboration			
Relationships With Teachers			

Sample Questions for Learning Rounds

#1 Orientation	#2 Activation	#3 Collaboration	#4 Relationships With Teachers
• Where are you going in your learning right now?	• What does a good learner look like in our class?	• How do you prefer to learn—on your own or with your peers?	• Do you get the same messages about learning from different teachers?
• What is your goal?	• What happens if you make a mistake in your class?	• Do you help others with their learning? How?	• Do your teachers help you understand what you're learning? How?
• Where are you now in your learning? How do you know your performance level?	• Are you a good learner? Why or why not? If you're not a good learner, can you become one?	• How do you know that the feedback you are giving is accurate?	• Do you feel that your teacher has high expectations for your learning? Does your teacher think that you can do really hard work?
• What next step do you need to take to improve your learning?	• What do the best learners in your class do differently from other learners?	• How do you know the feedback you are receiving is accurate?	• Do you think your teacher likes being a teacher? What do you think they like best?
• How do you improve your learning? How do you know if you are improving?	• How can you recognize the best learners in the class?	• How do you feel about feedback?	• Does your teacher give you a chance to decide what and how you're learning?
• How will you know you learned something?	• Are the best learners the same as the people who get the highest marks?	• How do you work with others to solve problems together?	• How does your teacher mainly teach you? (e.g., talking to the whole class, giving group tasks)
• What do you need to do next in order to learn ____?	• Should learning be easy or hard? Why?	• How do you feel about being in teams or groups? Why?	• Do you feel like you can ask this teacher for help when you don't understand how to do something?
• Do you understand how your learning is assessed?	• What do you do when you get stuck?	• Are there any things that your peers could do to help you learn more?	• Can you tell me about a time when this teacher really helped you learn something?
• Do you always know what you are learning and why?	• What happens if you make a mistake in class?	• Are there any things that you could do to help your peers learn more?	• Does your teacher explain to you what you need to do to make progress with your learning?
• What are you learning to do in art/health/math/English/science/etc. at the moment? How will you know when you have learned it?	• What strategies do you use when you're lost? What do you do when you don't know what to do?	• Can you tell me about a time when your peers really helped you learn something?	
• How do you track your performance?	• What strategies do you use when you're first learning something (surface)?	• How can others push your thinking?	
• How do you talk about different levels of difficulty in learning?		• What feedback do you seek to improve your learning?	

(Continued)

(Continued)

#1 Orientation	#2 Activation	#3 Collaboration	#4 Relationships With Teachers
• What are the expectations at each level of complexity (surface, deep, transfer)?	• What strategies do you use when you're proficient (deep)? • What strategies do you use to go beyond or to apply your learning (transfer)? • What enables learners to persevere? • How do you learn? • What enables learners to recognize their successes and challenges? • What helps learners stay focused? • What strategies do you use when you're bored? Are you bored often?	• How can others strengthen or challenge your ideas? • How do you push someone's thinking forward without telling them what you want them to do? • How do you collectively press forward and co-construct new ideas and solutions with peers? • How do you celebrate and challenge your individual ideas to create a better solution together? • How do you support others in pulling their thinking forward? • How do you pull someone's learning forward? • How do you pause your thinking and listen to others? • How do you pause on your first response and think deeply about supporting others? • How do you "stay soft on people" and "hard on content"? • What strategies do you use when you disagree? Or feel indifferent? • How do you support others in pulling their thinking forward? • How do you pull someone's learning forward?	• Does your teacher challenge you to achieve at a high level? • Do your classmates behave well for this teacher? Why or why not? • Does this teacher give you feedback about your learning? How? • Do your teachers help you with "how" to learn as well as "what" to learn? How?

Prompts for Discussion

What?	So What?	Now What?
• What did you notice about their understanding about where they were in their learning? • What did you notice about their ability to self-regulate their learning? • What did you notice about their attitudes toward getting something wrong or not understanding? • What did you notice about their feelings and ability to give and receive feedback? • What strategies emerged from learners in taking ownership over their own learning? • What stood out for you regarding student and teacher relationships?	• What story are you telling yourself right now about these learners? What is another narrative we could be telling right now? • What inferences can we draw about student orientation, activation, and collaboration?	• In light of this data, what next steps can we take? • Who will do ___ (what) by when? • Do we need to stop doing something good to do these next steps? What will we stop doing?

ACTIVITY 5.5: CREATING THE RIGHT MEETING

Several lead teachers have come to you and are concerned that the time the staff is spending on creating unit and lessons plans is taking teachers away from focusing on student learning and classroom-based intervention. How would you structure a series of meetings to address this concern and the numerous questions that will likely emerge?

NEXT STEPS

1. Redesignate your meeting structures to relate to the levels of meeting discussions discussed in this chapter.

2. Conduct a CFT audit using the CFT success criteria discussed in this chapter. The key areas of a CFT include

   a. inspecting their impact on learning,

   b. identifying potential next steps that would improve learning, and

   c. reviewing learning theories and relationship to teacher actions (see the end of the next chapter for learning principles and references).

3. Engage in a learning rounds process with teachers and share key findings with staff. How did the focus change in each of the areas of the rounds process: problem of practice, observation of practice, observation debrief, and next level of work?

What?	So What?	Now What?

6

Crafting

The Lead Learner

To make a substantial impact on student and staff learning, educational leaders need to have a laser focus on establishing clarity, coherence, and capacity building across their system. It is truly that simple and yet is incredibly difficult to execute. One reason for this difficulty is that leaders face competing beliefs regarding what students should learn, how they learn, and the purpose for educational institutions. The beliefs that leaders possess fundamentally influence how they approach their decisions and impact the design of the organization, the actions of staff, and the resulting learning of both staff and students. This issue requires leaders to think deeply about these beliefs, then articulate a narrative that enables others to make sense of the various opinions, myths, biases, and facts that permeate education systems and then make decisions that are in the best interests of students. Furthermore, the lead learner must use strategies in his or her own daily lives that model the practices that staff should be using to impact staff and student learning. As this book has shown, this requires an ambidextrous approach of standardizing criteria for learning and customizing the approach for ensuring everyone learns at high levels.

Crafting embodies the idea of the lead learner continually designing a narrative that enables others to focus and make sense of what is critically important in educational organizations—the substantial growth in learning for all. By establishing this focus, educators will have the ability to establish clarity of expectations, ensure coherence of systems, and enhance capacity of faculty to continually refine and develop in their work. Moreover, crafting embodies the idea of the lead learner using personal leadership strategies that cause learning for themselves and the people they influence daily. For example, the lead learner must visualize the thinking of others. They do this by establishing agreements in social situations that explore assumptions, test ideas, and make decisions that move learning forward.

This chapter begins by exploring these competing beliefs and highlighting how the lead learner navigates these tensions and establishes a narrative of sensemaking to others. This chapter then moves to specific strategies that leaders use on a daily basis to move staff and student learning forward.

Facing Competing Beliefs in Learning

All educational leaders are faced with a series of questions that implicitly and/or explicitly drive a number of decisions that have a substantial impact on the learning of children and staff. The lead learner is aware of the ubiquitous and often latent nature of these questions and the importance of bringing these questions to the forefront of other staff members to provide a narrative of learning for all. A sample set of such questions are provided below:

QUESTION I: DO STUDENTS NEED FACTUAL KNOWLEDGE or *DO STUDENTS AND TEACHERS NEED A SET OF SOCIAL AND COGNITIVE SKILLS IN THE 21ST CENTURY?*
Yong Zhao (2012) argues that, "For too long, students have been passive consumers and recipients of whatever adults give them: books, facilities, knowledge, tests, and disciplines. Schools have been built to facilitate effective consumption and create great recipients rather than makers, creators, and entrepreneurs" (p. 209). One could read Zhao's point of view as stating that factual knowledge within core academic disciplines is of relatively less importance than creativity and entrepreneurship. School leaders who embrace this point of view will focus their efforts on deep learning methodologies (i.e., problem- and project-based learning), creative learning spaces (i.e., open space, adaptive learning environments), and courses that infuse massive technology use.

But consider the work of Daniel Willingham (2009), who wrote, "trying to teach students skills such as analysis or synthesis in the absence of factual knowledge is impossible. Research from cognitive science has shown that the sort of skills that teachers want for students—such as the ability to analyze and to think critically—*require* extensive factual knowledge." In other words, *facts precede skill*. This makes intuitive sense; we cannot think critically about something we do not understand. Willingham (2017) also says that children cannot just conduct online searches to find answers to questions because children need to understand the actual context of terms and concepts and where to apply those concepts in their work. This requires knowing basic facts and skills, relating those concepts and skills, and then applying ideas across contexts.

> *Lead learner's response:* A basis of core knowledge and skills is required to utilize critical-thinking skills and social-emotional skills. The accumulation of knowledge without the purpose of developing critical thinking and means for self- and social management is monotonous and counterproductive to learning and reinvesting in learning.

QUESTION II: SHOULD STUDENTS OWN THEIR LEARNING INDEPENDENTLY or SHOULD THE TEACHER DIRECT THE LEARNING?

"Kids can teach themselves." In 2007, Sugata Mitra argued that the natural curiosity of children and their innate ability to acquire a significant level of knowledge without adult prompting moved learning forward. A computer was placed in the slums of one of the largest cities in India. Children who had never seen a computer came across the device. Over time, children became proficient in using the device and learning content without adult intervention, or what Mitra calls, "minimally invasive education." Mitra makes a compelling case that with independence, collaboration with peers, and a bit of encouragement children can emerge as the creative people they were destined to be. Interestingly, the net yield of academic literacy was approximately 40–60% of the desired level of competency.

In *Rigorous PBL by Design* (McDowell, 2017), Stonefields School was highlighted as a school that focused on taking a hands-on approach to developing a student's ability to "own their own learning" (i.e., to monitor, regulate, and improve their own learning). Moreover, schools such as Ross School provide differentiated support to students based on their level of understanding. A general rule of thumb is more directive approaches are used at the earlier stages of learning whereas more inquiry-based approaches emerge as students are approaching mastery.

> *Lead learner's response:* For someone to own their own learning they must learn how to learn, developing the knowledge and skills necessary to measure their own learning and identifying next steps in problem solving which, of course, requires both direction and autonomy. Moreover, this requires time as learners need deliberate and continuous practice over time to develop mastery. Specific strategies that enhance learning often vary at surface, deep, and transfer levels.

QUESTION III: DO STUDENTS LEARN FROM THEIR PEERS or DO THEY LEARN INDEPENDENTLY?

One of the most important findings in education research is that 80% of the feedback kids receive is from their friends and the majority of that feedback is incorrect (Nuthall, 2007). This finding illuminates the importance of peer influence and the social nature of learning. Students learn vast amounts from social examples, classroom discussion, and as mentioned, peer-to-peer feedback.

Interestingly, we also know that certain strategies support learners at lower levels of complexity of learning that are far less collaborative than deeper levels of understanding. Moreover, research has also shown that when students are by themselves they develop a higher number and variety of solutions than with peers in groups and/or teams (Chamorro-Premuzic, 2015), although groups are critical for solidification of ideas.

> *Lead learner's response:* Learning from others is incredibly powerful in enhancing learning. Peers and experts that provide feedback, modeling, and direct instruction are invaluable for learning. How educators structure how people learn (individually or in a group) depends largely on what people already know (prior knowledge) and the accuracy of feedback that others are prepared to provide (student and teacher clarity).

QUESTION IV: DO STUDENTS LEARN KNOWLEDGE AND SKILLS DIFFERENTLY IN THE 21ST CENTURY or DO THEY LEARN THE SAME WAY THEY ALWAYS HAVE?

As technology has continued to become more a way of life for people in the way they shop, communicate, study, and engage in education, many people have argued that children today think and process information differently than people prior to the technology revolution (or revolutions). An idea that has existed for a while now is that globalization and technology has fundamentally changed the way students actually learn (e.g., "the digital native"). Beyond such general claims, further arguments have been made regarding the specific individual differences of every child providing a renewed life for "learning styles" (e.g., kinesthetic, auditory, and visual learners) and ultimately personalized learning (i.e., the teaching style/format fits their preferred learning style).

The challenge here is that these arguments run aground against how the brain actually works (Hattie & Yates, 2014). Though changes in the format of classes, the ways in which students can access information and gain feedback have changed, the way people learn has not substantially changed over time.

> *Lead learner's response:* There are two main ideas at play here. The first idea is how information is accessed in the 21st century. The second is how people learn in the 21st century. The challenge is that these often get conflated. In the 21st century, people can access information in a variety of ways (i.e., social media, Wikipedia, Google, experts in class, peer groups) and at any time of the day. Simultaneously, the way in which people learn, that is how information is internalized into long-term memory, has not changed in the 21st century. Children are more alike in how they learn than we recognize, and every human being understands new ideas and skills in the context of what they already know. Finding out what kids already know and then providing support beyond their current understanding is critical for their learning.

QUESTION V: ARE STUDENTS MOTIVATED BY EMOTIONAL OR COGNITIVE ENGAGEMENT?

Connecting academic content and classroom tasks to student interest and passion has long been a goal of educators. Relating student work to contemporary events is a critical element attempting to sustain student motivation by evoking a sense of emotional engagement for the duration of the unit. This is particularly true for inquiry-based instructional models. Research has shown that a primary motivator for learning comes about when a cognitive gap is revealed when new ideas conflict with our existing knowledge (McDowell, 2017). Connecting academic content and classroom tasks to student misconceptions and prior knowledge has emerged in the literature recently as key to the type of engagement that is necessary to engage students and move their learning forward (Muller, 2008).

> *Lead learner's response:* Emotional engagement is incredibly powerful for short-term goals but lacks the staying power of cognitive engagement. Lead learners believe that both approaches should be utilized where cognitive engagement should be specifically articulated to staff and students throughout the learning process.

QUESTION VI: ARE SCHOOLS RESPONSIBLE FOR ENSURING THAT ALL STUDENTS ATTAIN AT LEAST ONE YEAR OF LEARNING GROWTH EACH YEAR or ARE SCHOOLS ONLY RESPONSIBLE FOR PROVIDING THE OPPORTUNITY FOR STUDENTS TO LEARN?

This question goes to the heart of our beliefs associated with children and their ability to learn at various levels of complexity (i.e., surface, deep, and transfer learning) and the role and responsibility of schools to move that learning forward. The literature is clear that socioeconomic status has a substantial effect on student learning and that what students bring to school produces the greatest variance in learning (Hattie, 2009). This same literature also shows the tremendous influence that teachers can have on student learning (well above the effect of socioeconomic status). How educators answer this question fundamentally influences the actions they take and ultimately the impact they have on their systems and on learning. For some, the focus on tracking, ability grouping, and structural changes such as scheduling and class structures appears to grant the greatest opportunities for learning but it lacks the research necessary for moving learning forward at a substantial rate.

> *Lead learner's response:* All students should have the opportunity and the appropriate interventions to make more than one year's growth in one year's time. The research is clear that the influences that are within the control of schools have a high likelihood of moving such learning forward. Our job is to unapologetically cause learning for all students.

Lead Learner Practices That Move Learning Forward

Lead learners cut through the aforementioned tensions and focus squarely on beliefs and actions that substantially move student and adult learning forward. To ensure all students and adults learn to high levels, lead learners must establish clarity, develop coherence, and build capacity. Moreover, lead learners must approach this development by using standardized and customizable approaches to move learning forward for all. Lastly, this requires lead learners to model in their daily practices effective teaching and learning by establishing common agreements for learning, leveraging protocols for dialogue, and modeling current initiatives in practice.

VOICES FROM THE FIELD

Rick Bagley, Superintendent

Ross Valley School District

San Anselmo, California

As I reflect upon my four decades-long journey in public education, one personal conclusion is that leadership seems ever-changing and evolving. Another conclusion is, no matter how much I think I've learned about leadership from mentors, books, research, or real-world experience, I'll forever be its humble and wide-eyed student.

Throughout the years I've been privileged to know, observe, work alongside, and learn from some of most amazing individuals, each of whom I consider to be outstanding leaders in their own right, no matter their role or position title. From school board trustees to maintenance workers, parents, community members, and especially students, these leaders continuously help define and refine what leadership has come to mean in this time and place, to me as a superintendent.

My best synthesis of all these many data points is that a great deal of the art and science of effective leadership today involves striking a precarious balance between charting a course and sticking to it, while at the same time being open to fresh ideas, new possibilities, and impactful innovations that might ultimately need to alter that course. On the surface this notion of leadership may seem paradoxical, yet I've come to believe through my own practical experience that alone these actions can either render an organization enslaved to outdated, irrelevant and ineffective practices, or perpetually chasing the latest panacea without ever staying long enough with anything to achieve meaningful and measurable results.

Establishing Common Agreements for Learning

Agreements are established norms of how people behave when working together to discuss ideas, make decisions, and to solve problems. The research is clear that certain agreements or norms enhance individual and collective learning (Argyris, 1977). Lead learners are intentional in establishing and using agreements that have a high likelihood of causing learning. For example, Figure 6.1 illustrates key learning principles that the lead learner wants to ensure are being practiced with their teams.

The lead learner structures his or her work with others (e.g., one-on-one conversations, meetings) to leverage the learning principles expressed in Figure 6.1. One way they do this is by establishing

Figure 6.1 Sample Learning Principles That Drive the Lead Learner Decision-Making

Learning Principle	Description
Deliberate Practice	Deliberate and continuous practice over time is necessary to develop mastery. As one practices and gains expertise, new strategies are needed to enhance learning at surface, deep, and transfer levels. Such practices are successful when one is thinking about the surface, deep, and transfer knowledge and skills expected while completing tasks.
Prior Knowledge	Children understand new things in the context of things they already know. Activating their prior knowledge and providing opportunities beyond what they know is ideal.
Cognitive Load	To think well on a concept or topic, factual knowledge must be developed first before complex thinking may emerge. The same goes for developing skills over time. Additionally, skills are more effectively acquired when factual knowledge is developed.
Social Learning	Learning from others is incredibly powerful in enhancing learning. Peers and experts that provide feedback, modeling, and direct instruction are invaluable for learning.
(Re)-Investing in Learning	Understanding and developing dispositions for learning enables people to meet short-term/long-term goals, which often affect human emotions.

Source: Derived from Bjork & Bjork, 2014; Hattie & Donoghue, 2016; Hattie & Yates, 2014; and Willingham, 2009.

agreements or norms for how people engage in dialogue on learning. Figure 6.2 articulates several agreements that the lead leader may use to operationalize identified learning principles.

Figure 6.2 Agreements That Drive Learning

Sample Agreements	Learning Principle	Rationale
Use questions to address potential conflicts and to explore ideas.	Social Learning	The lead learner uses questions to explore ideas, give and receive feedback, and mine for conflict in social situations to develop collective understanding and move forward in decision-making.
Always check in on each member of the group to make sure they understand each other.	Cognitive Load	The lead learner consistently monitors group member knowledge and skills so they may find ways to support others in developing key knowledge and skills to move forward and to prepare members to engage in cognitively challenging conversations in the future.
Each group member will explain their actions or beliefs to the group.	(Re)-Investing in Learning	The lead learner models and expects that everyone shares their rationale for opinions, positions, and decisions they made so that everyone may understand the personal and professional assumptions, inferences, and interests that drive decision-making.
Each group member is responsible for all other group members in understanding the task and coaching each other to perform at a high level.	Deliberate Practice	The lead learner recognizes that without practice team members will be unable to develop mastery. The following agreement supports staff in assisting others in engaging in high-impact practices.

(Continued)

Figure 6.2   (Continued)

Sample Agreements	Learning Principle	Rationale
Each group member will explain important words and provide specific examples when needed.	Cognitive Load Social Learning	The lead learner develops habits within groups to define and articulate core concepts amongst staff members to ensure everyone has the same understanding before moving toward decision-making.
When sharing ideas all members will advocate their ideas and ask questions about other ideas.	Social Learning Prior Knowledge	The lead learner establishes an expectation whereby people argue for their interests while also listening to others for feedback and different viewpoints.

Leverage Protocols for Dialogue

Lead learners use a series of protocols (or structural devices) to make collective decisions. A protocol is simply a routine for engaging in an activity or task. For example, the Critical Friends protocol (see the Appendix) serves as a way for a large group of people to give feedback to others on their current thinking, a product, or a particular strategy. The protocol is intended to provide efficiency in giving feedback from a large group of people while also ensuring that those receiving the feedback do not feel personally criticized. In other words, critical friends teams serve as a way to be "soft on people," hence "friends," and "hard on content," hence "critical."

Based on the types of decisions leaders need to make, protocols can be used to enable groups to explore ideas and possibilities (i.e., divergent approaches) as well select one of several possibilities (i.e., convergent approaches) to make a decision (see Figure 6.3).

Model Current Initiatives in Daily Practice

Throughout this book, lead learners have taken an ambidextrous perspective (balanced between a standardized and customizable

Figure 6.3 Protocols

Approach	Protocols
Convergent	• Critical Friends • What?, So What?, Now What? • SWOT Analysis • Pareto Chart • Criteria Development • Boundary Setting Mission Management • Force Field Analysis • Stakeholder Analysis
Divergent	• Feedback Carousel • Leadership/Consultancy Dilemma • Metaphor • Mind Map • Tree Diagram • Future Protocol • Personal Power Grid • Zones of Comfort, Risk, and Danger

approach) to developing systems that ensure high levels of learning for staff and students. Lead learners focus on standardizing and scaling success criteria for professional learning, instruction, and personnel systems while optimizing customization in the approach of how teachers learn, how they teach, and how people are selected for the organizations.

The lead learner must "model" the practices that teachers and staff are required to execute on a daily basis. This means that leaders must engage in professional learning with staff and adhere to the criteria of effective professional learning. Potential ways of doing this are specified in Figure 6.4.

Figure 6.4 Lead Learner Actions

• Participate in professional learning with staff
• Articulate the learning intentions and success criteria of faculty meetings: What does the meeting intend to convey? How will the success of the meeting be measured?
• Find out what staff knows before, during, and after the meeting.
• Check in with staff during the meeting to see if they are understanding the concept at hand; if they are not, alter your delivery method appropriately.

VOICES FROM THE FIELD

Sascha Heckmann, Director at American International School of Mozambique

"Embrace the paradox!" has been a mantra that I have used throughout my leadership journey. I am fully aware that my profession exists to prepare children for their future yet we invariably end up preparing kids for their parents' past. Content knowledge, accuracy, compliance, sorting and selecting, tests—these are all legacies that comfort our community but put student future readiness in jeopardy. In embracing the paradox, I have found myself empowered as a leader to push my schools beyond the past while acknowledging its value in the journey for those working in our schools. . . . My leadership journey has been defined by the ability to embrace the best of a 20th-century education by making it the minimum, or floor, of expectation, and then inspiring our school community to reach beyond our notion of a 21st century to create future-ready, lifelong learners.

CONCLUSION

The lead learner establishes a narrative that focuses the organization on learning and learning at high levels for everyone. In Chapter 2, the lead learner did this by establishing clarity in the strategic planning process. In this chapter, the lead leader accomplishes this work by implementing daily practices associated with creating agreements, utilizing protocols, and direct modeling.

Lead learners are agnostic about types of instruction delivery—rather than focus on one particular method of delivering instruction, instead they focus on the outcomes: Are students learning? How does the instructional method need to be altered to ensure more effective and efficient learning? Such lead learners anchor their work on cognitive science and develop systems that orient educators to solve problems around student learning. Lead learners support systems in this work by establishing a compelling narrative about learning for all and engaging everyone in conversations that are often challenging but necessary to improve systems. Lead learners use protocols that assist in amplifying the message, opening up dialogue, and taking next steps for kids.

REFLECTION QUESTIONS

1. How would you craft your skills to become or continue developing as a lead learner?

2. Identify one of the three areas of the lead learner that is a *strength* for you. Why do you think that?

3. Identify one of the three areas of the lead learner that is a *challenge* or *area of growth* for you. Explain.

ACTIVITIES

ACTIVITY 6.1: ALIGNING ACTIONS WITH ASPIRATIONS

Brainstorm a particular leadership focus that would promote the learning principles to live by for students and staff. Several examples have been provided below.

Figure 6.5 Aligning Leadership Actions With Learning Principles

Learning Principle	Description	Leadership Focus
Deliberate Practice	Deliberate and continuous practice over time is necessary to develop mastery. As one practices and gains expertise, new strategies are needed to enhance learning at surface, deep, and transfer levels. Such practices are successful when one is thinking about the surface, deep, and transfer knowledge and skills expected while completing tasks.	• Establish learning intentions and success criteria for key learning outcomes at surface, deep, and transfer levels. • Engage CFTs in reviewing learning, instruction, and feedback strategies with students at surface, deep, and transfer levels.
Prior Knowledge	Children are more alike than different in terms of learning, and as such they understand new things in the context of things they already know. Activating their prior knowledge and providing opportunities beyond what they know is ideal.	• Invest in pre-assessments as part of the learning–teaching process. • Invest in formative assessment practices. • Develop a learning-system infrastructure.

(Continued)

Figure 6.5 (Continued)

Learning Principle	Description	Leadership Focus
Cognitive Load	To think well on a concept or topic, factual knowledge must be developed first before complex thinking may emerge. The same goes for developing skills over time. Additionally, skills are more effectively acquired when factual knowledge is developed.	• Embed 21st-century skill learning intentions and success criteria within core academic areas. • Provide professional development experiences for faculty that enables staff to juxtapose 21st-century skills and content-based strategies. • Ensure that students are engaging in developing their factual understanding prior to or simultaneously with the development of skills.
Social Learning	Learning from others is incredibly powerful in enhancing learning. Peers and experts that provide feedback, modeling, and direct instruction are invaluable for learning.	• Provide professional development experiences for faculty that enable staff to continually develop their feedback skills, develop student peer-to-peer feedback skills, and enhance instructional strategies.
(Re)-Investing in Learning	Understanding and developing dispositions for learning enables people to meet short-term/long-term goals that often affect human emotions and require different instructional and learning strategies.	• Embed learning intentions and success criteria within core academic areas. • Provide professional development experiences for faculty that enables staff to juxtapose conative, cognitive, and content-based strategies. • Clarify instructional, feedback, and learning strategies that enhance student learning.

ACTIVITY 6.2: FOCUS OF GROWTH

Identify one action that you are interested in working on as a lead learner this year:

- Participate in professional learning with staff.
- Articulate the learning intentions and success criteria of faculty meetings: What does the meeting intend to convey? How will the success of the meeting be measured?
- Find out what staff knows before, during, and after the meeting.
- Check in with staff during the meeting to see if they are understanding the concept at hand; if they are not, alter your delivery method appropriately.

Next, identify what ways you will practice, receive feedback, and track your own growth in learning. Share this plan with staff and use the Critical Friends protocol to receive feedback.

NEXT STEPS

1. Identify those areas that you want to craft and that you think your organization requires. Narrow that list to one specific action that you will focus on for the next several months.

2. Have your team review their own needs and strategies that would improve their practice. (Gentle reminder: Have staff collect evidence before making a decision—let evidence drive action!)

3. Review the "learning principles to live by" with staff and identify ways to support educators in using those principles when analyzing data, making inferences, and identifying next steps. Do the same with administrators in how such principles guide (or should guide) processes/procedures, systems, and structures. Finally, do the same for students in understanding those principles in their daily lives.

7

Conclusion

In 2013, Malcolm Gladwell wrote a story about the Karnaphuli Paper Mills in East Asia. The paper mill was built to process the bamboo from nearby forests; however, the bamboo died in a unique, once-in-a-50-year phenomenon. As he states, "Dead bamboo was useless for pulping; it fell apart as it was floated down the river." However, the operators of the mill developed new supply chains, established a research program to create faster-growing species of bamboo, and began experimenting with new tracts of bamboo. He continues, "They found other kinds of lumber that worked just as well. The result was that the plant was blessed with a far more diversified base of raw materials than had ever been imagined."

The story of the mill can be considered from both a learning and a leadership standpoint. The people in the mill integrated creativity and pragmatism brought forward by a strong knowledge base in core content *and* a level of collaboration and critical thinking. The people running the paper mills had to (1) understand substantial content knowledge in forestry, botany, and management and operations; furthermore, (2) mill operators had to be willing to think critically and creatively to come up with innovative solutions to a new problem. The ability to engage in this type of ambidextrous problem solving is *critical* for our children. Students need to have mastery of core content knowledge, the confidence to handle setbacks, and the creative and social wherewithal to develop solutions when problems emerge. This practice of ambidextrous problem solving is best modeled by lead learners. Lead learners establish standard approaches to ensure that students acquire needed skills while also diversifying the ways in which such knowledge and skills are acquired and assessed.

Lead learners focus the work of educators on student and staff learning. They structure their decision-making so that educators maximize their time solving problems of learning. They do this by

- standardizing the focus of the institution and the work of the organization (clarity),
- aligning educational and human systems to promote and engage great people in practices that move learning forward (coherence),
- adhering to a set of key criteria for professional learning (capacity), and
- crafting a narrative and set of personal leadership skills that enable others to make sense of, focus on, and increase learning for all.

Lead learners do not have a blueprint for the right lesson plans, instructional approaches, textbooks, classroom structures, or even who, when, and how people work together to solve problems. It is the nexus between this defined autonomy that is critical in complex organizations to thrive and develop. Lead learners craft a skill set that models this work by laying out agreements that leverage learning, protocols that catalyze conversations associated with problem solving, and modeling practices that move students forward and illustrate a commitment to effective teaching and learning (see Figure 7.1).

Figure 7.1   Key Design Shifts: Aligning Leadership and Teaching High-Impact Focus

Teacher Focus	Leader Focus
• **Clarity:** Students need to be absolutely clear on what they are expected to learn, where they are in their learning, and what next steps they need to take to advance their learning.	• **Clarity:** Leaders need to be absolutely clear on the key outcomes of a learning organization (to ensure more than one year's growth in one year's time in content and 21st-century skills across surface, deep, and transfer expectations), where the organization is currently in meeting those outcomes, and specific next steps to improve learning for all.

Teacher Focus	Leader Focus
• **Coherence:** Students need to have a consistent balance of surface, deep, and transfer knowledge and to thoroughly understand and apply content to real-world challenging problems. Each level of content complexity requires different instructional interventions, tasks, and feedback.	• **Coherence:** Leaders need to ensure that all systems are aligned to meet the specific outcomes of the organization and the right people are in place to make decisions on the strategies and approaches necessary for moving learning forward in their context.
• **Capacity:** Students need to be able to talk about their learning, monitor their learning, advocate for next steps in their learning, and be a part of a culture that focuses on, supports, and models such efforts.	• **Capacity:** Leaders need to ensure that all staff engage in the work of student learning, monitor their impact on student learning, advocate for next steps in their impact on learning, and be a part of a team that focuses on and builds knowledge and skills around such efforts.

Moving Beyond Stark Differences

Lead learners rise beyond the current debate concerning 20th- vs. 21st-century education and transformational vs. instructional leadership and instead anchor their work solely on the learning of children and staff. In her book *Little Soldiers* (2017), Lenora Chu argues that the United States' educational system needs to take lessons learned from other countries like China in how they prepare children for academic rigor and maintain the American success of student creativity and entrepreneurship. In a radio interview with KQED, Chu argued that the way Steve Jobs is viewed in both countries is strikingly different (Kim, 2017). Americans view him as a creative innovator whereas the Chinese view him as someone with massive amounts of knowledge. Both are right and wrong in that he was clearly both. Rather than falling into step with the either/or mentality of the public debate at large, we as educators need to lead the way by embracing the valuable strategies found in multiple strains of educational schools of thought. We can do this successfully in our schools by ensuring clarity, creating coherence, building capacity, and crafting our personal leadership skills using both a standardized and customizable approach to move learning forward for all students.

Influencing Educators

The ambidextrous approach to learning and teaching is highly motivating for both educators and students. Several scholars have noted that today's workforce demands situations where they are solving authentic problems, using data to drive decision-making, and finding work that makes tangible changes within the larger organization or society (Wagner, 2012; Wiliam, 2011; Zhao, 2012). As such, lead learners are attracted to people and environments where meaningful tasks, constant collaboration, and competency-enhancing opportunities are provided, and problem-solving situations are present.

The main challenges are (and always will be) *how do we ensure that all students are getting one year's growth in one year's time in content and 21st-century skills? How do we ensure that students are developing surface-, deep-, and transfer-level learning?* Educational systems will "never arrive" in meeting these questions. There is no silver bullet, no cavalry coming to answer the questions. No, these questions will be constantly worked on and the solutions that are identified will be helpful to support the organization as it develops. Interestingly, as lead learners go down this path, one of the greatest challenges they face is the demand and speed in which structural changes will always challenge their approach to educating children.

Recognizing the Rate of Change

One of the greatest challenges leaders face is that creative ideas spread faster than routine, pragmatic ideas. On July 29, 2013, Atul Gawande illuminated in his *New Yorker* article *Slow Ideas* that the pace of innovations spreading across the medical field varied dramatically. Interestingly, he found that innovations, such as anesthesia, permeated the medical field and scaled at a rapid pace. Such an innovation was attractive to doctors as they no longer had the arduous task of holding patients down to conduct surgery or watching patients go through tremendous agony. Such an innovation had a direct personal benefit to the doctor and reduced the taxing environment in the operating room. Patients benefited as well, having the omnipresent relief of "going to sleep" rather than being exposed to the pain of surgery. Handwashing, however, continues in contemporary medical institutions to be a difficult innovation to infuse and sustain. There is clearly a benefit to handwashing, but it is a painful, cumbersome, daily routine for doctors. For this innovation to scale and sustain over time, specific protocols and training programs have to be established, and most importantly, daily conversations with coworkers must be held to hold one another responsible for this impactful innovation to occur. The lead learners realize that learning intentions and success criteria, feedback, and critical friends teams are akin to handwashing— necessary but laborious and not glorious.

As you prepare to go back into your school or district and lead the change, approach the work from both innovation and rigor. This is critical because we have to get past the notion of catching up to China, Finland, and the like or leading the way for 21st-century education and see that we can catch up in some ways (perhaps some of our basic skills) and continue to lead in other skills ways. The way forward is to do tiny decent things: to establish clarity, develop coherence, build capacity, and craft skills that substantially moves learning forward for every child.

Epilogue

Over the years, I have seen many district leaders go after the shiny new toy, only to find out that the toy is neither shiny nor new. All the chasing brought them back to the same starting point, with a much larger sense of frustration. All of this chasing and frustration can lead to the resentment of staff, and they become leery of the next initiative that comes their way. What they need most of all is to understand their current reality, and then take time to understand what it is that they really need. What I enjoyed about Michael McDowell's approach is that he wants us to focus on our current reality, and he articulates well that our current reality should always be focused on learning, as opposed to all of the adult issues that can take place in school.

For full disclosure, I have not always enjoyed the term *lead learner* because too many of those in charge set the course in isolation, move forward, and then work to bring others on board with them—another missed opportunity, because people want to be involved from the beginning, and not at the middle. We all know that for any improvement to work, we must all carry the learning from time to time, and this is why McDowell has helped changed my mind a bit when it comes to the term lead learner. He does not believe that all of this should be the responsibility of one person, but it should be the shared responsibility of staff, students, and families.

As someone who works with leaders in many countries, I find that what often happens is that we talk about changes necessary, and use educational words to back up what we think, but we don't take the time to discuss how we can build a common understanding together before we move on. McDowell helps us solve that issue before it begins, and he always maintains the student focus.

In this book, McDowell laid out the need for clarity, coherence, and capacity for all, and then he provided step-by-step instructions of how to go about doing that. There are graphs, charts, talking points, and reflection questions, all of which lead us to a deeper understanding. I like when a book can be used as a resource, where we go back often to revisit how we are moving forward, and helps us take time to make sure we have clarity in our movements forward. What I enjoyed the most is that he seems to understand all of the stakeholders in a school community and helps us reflect on how to meet their needs.

An additional strength of the book is that McDowell utilizes the vast research from John Hattie, someone we both work with as Visible Learning trainers. However, he does more than just tout the research— McDowell has a deep understanding of it and how it can help us move forward. He sees the "what" and the "how" of a system's change. And, as would be expected, he always brings us back to students and learning.

What I like most about McDowell's book is not always what he writes, but what he, in fact, does as a school district leader. Many times throughout the book he writes that we should "stay small and stay focused." I remember Pasi Sahlberg, author of *Finnish Lessons* and *FinnishED Leadership,* say that, "to rush educational change is to ruin it," and "use small data to make big change." McDowell uses a similar thought process because too often we can get lost in the big data and plethora of evidence that surrounds us. McDowell's constant phrase of "stay small and stay focused" is an important message that we need to pay attention to as we move forward with our initiatives. It provides us with a beacon to help guide us to our initial mission.

I hope you noticed that McDowell did not offer "five easy steps" or "five simple solutions," and I appreciate that. Anyone who is a leader or has spent time in leadership will tell you that preparing our students for their future is not an easy lift, but it is a worthy one. It takes a leader who understands the needs of both student and adult learners, and that is what McDowell did with this important book.

Peter M. DeWitt, EdD
Author/Consultant
Finding Common Ground **blog (***Education Week***)**

References

Agile Schools Pty Ltd. (n.d.). *About learning sprints* [Video featuring Dr. Simon Breakspear]. Retrieved from http://www.agileschools.com/about-learning-sprints/

Ambidextrous. (2017). In *Merriam-Webster dictionary*. Retrieved from https://www.merriam-webster.com/dictionary/ambidextrous

Argyris, C. (1977). *Double loop learning in organizations*. Cambridge, MA: Harvard Business Review.

Argyris, C., Putnam, R., & McLain Smith, D. (1985). *Action science: Concepts, methods, and skills for research and intervention*. San Francisco, CA: Jossey-Bass.

Bjork, E. L., & Bjork, R. A. (2014). Making things hard on yourself, but in a good way: Creating desirable difficulties to enhance learning. In M. A. Gernsbacher & J. Pomerantz (Eds.), *Psychology and the real world: Essays illustrating fundamental contributions to society* (2nd ed.; pp. 59–68). New York, NY: Worth.

Brookfield, S. D. (1986). *Understanding and facilitating adult learning. A comprehensive analysis of principles and effective practices*. San Francisco, CA: Jossey-Bass.

Capra, F. (1975). *The tao of physics*. New York, NY: HarperCollins.

Capra, F. (1988). *Uncommon wisdom: Conversations with remarkable people*. New York, NY: Simon & Schuster.

Capra, F. (1997). *The web of life: A new scientific understanding of living systems*. New York, NY: Anchor.

Chamorro-Premuzic, T. (2015, March 25). Why group brainstorming is a waste of time. *Harvard Business Review*. Retrieved from http://hbr.org/2015/03/why-group-brainstorming-is-a-waste-of-time

Christensen, C. M. (1999). What is an organization's culture? *Harvard Business School Background Note 399–104*. (Revised August 2006.)

Chu, L. (2017). *Little soldiers: An American boy, a Chinese school, and the global race to achieve*. New York, NY: HarperCollins.

City, E. A., Elmore, R. F., Fiarman, S. E., & Teitel, L. (2009). *Instructional rounds in education: A network approach to improving teaching and learning*. Boston, MA: Harvard Education Press.

Eisenhower, D. D. (1957, November). *Remarks*. National Defense Reserve.

Fancher, L. (2013, January 30). Rejecting the 'best practices' of baseball: Billy Beane, Paul DePodesta tell 'Moneyball' success story. *Mercury News*. Retrieved from http://www.mercurynews.com/2013/01/30/rejecting-the-best-practices-of-baseball-billy-beane-paul-depodesta-tell-moneyball-success-story-2/

Gawande, A. (2013, July 29). Slow ideas: Some innovations spread fast. How do you speed the ones that don't. *The New Yorker*. Retrieved from https://www.newyorker.com/magazine/2013/07/29/slow-ideas

Gladwell, M. (2000, May 29). The new-boy network. *The New Yorker*.

Gladwell, M. (2013, June 24). The gift of doubt: Albert O. Hirschman and the power of failure. *The New Yorker*.

Gomez, J. (2017). *Progress and proficiency matrix for kids*. Ross, CA: Ross School District.

Goska, D. V. (2004, November). Political paralysis. *Sun Magazine*.

Hargreaves, A., Boyle, A., & Harris, A. (2014). *Uplifting leadership: How organizations, teams, and communities raise performance*. San Francisco, CA: Jossey-Bass.

Harmony Education Center, National School Reform Faculty. (2014). https://www.nsrfharmony.org/content/protocols

Harvey, T., Bearley, W., & Corkrum, S. (1997). *The practical decision maker: A handbook for decision making and problem solving in organizations*. London: R & L Education.

Hattie, J. (2009). *Visible learning: A synthesis of over 800 meta-analyses relating to achievement*. New York, NY: Routledge.

Hattie, J. (2011). *Visible learning: Maximizing impact on learning for teachers*. New York, NY: Routledge.

Hattie, J. (2012). *Visible learning for teachers*. New York, NY: Routledge.

Hattie, J., & Donoghue, G. (2016). Learning strategies: A synthesis and conceptual model. *npj Science of Learning*, 1. doi:10.1038/npjscilearn.2016.13

Hattie, J., & Timperley, H. (2007). The power of feedback. *Review of Educational Research, 77*(1), 81–112.

Hattie, J., & Yates, G. (2014). *Visible learning and the science of how we learn*. New York, NY: Routledge.

Kelley, T., & Kelley, D. (2013). *Creative confidence: Unleashing the creative potential within us all*. New York, NY: Crown Business.

Kim, Q. S. (Producer). (2017, September 20). *An inside look at China's education system* [Radio Program]. San Francisco, CA: KQED.

Kotter, J., & Cohen, D. (2002). *The heart of change*. Boston, MA: Harvard Business School Press.

Lewis, M. (2003). *Moneyball: The art of winning an unfair game*. New York: NY: W. W. Norton & Company.

Marzano, R. J. (2007). *The art and science of teaching: A comprehensive framework for effective instruction*. Alexandria, VA: ASCD.

Marzano, R. J. (2017). *The new art and science of teaching: More than fifty new instructional strategies for academic success*. Bloomington, IN: Solution Tree.

McDowell, M. (2017). *Rigorous PBL by design: Three shifts for developing confident and competent learners*. Thousand Oaks, CA: Corwin.

Mitra, S. (2007, February). *Sugata Mitra | LIFT 2007: Kids can teach themselves* [Video file].Retrieved from https://www.ted.com/talks/sugata_mitra_shows_how_kids_teach_themselves

Muhammad, A. (2009). *Transforming school culture: How to overcome staff division*. Bloomington, IN: Solution Tree.

Muller, D. A. (2008). *Designing effective multimedia for physics education* (Doctoral dissertation). Retrieved from http://physics.usyd.edu.au/super/theses/PhD(Muller).pdf

Nuthall, G. A. (2007). *The hidden lives of learners*. Wellington: New Zealand Council for Educational Research.

Pink, D. H. (2013). *To sell is human: The surprising truth about moving others*. New York, NY: Riverhead Books.

Reeves, D., & Flach, T. (2011). Data: Meaningful analysis can rescue schools from drowning in data. *Journal of Staff Development, 32*(4), 34–40.

Robinson, V. (2011). *Student-centered leadership*. San Francisco, CA: Jossey-Bass.

Robinson, V. M. J., Lloyd, C. A., & Rowe, K. J. (December 2008). The impact of leadership on student outcomes: An analysis of the differential effects of leadership. *Educational Administration Quarterly, 44*(5), 635–674.

Rolle, L. (2015). *Learning disposition dichotomy shift chart*. Elk Grove, CA: Reese Elementary School.

Schwarz, R. (2013). *Smart leaders, smarter teams: How you and your team get unstuck to get results*. San Francisco, CA: Jossey-Bass.

Schwarz, R. (2016). *The skilled facilitator: A comprehensive resource for consultants, facilitators, coaches and trainers* (3rd ed.). San Francisco, CA: Jossey-Bass.

Seidel, S. (2011). *Hip hop genius: Remixing high school education*. Lanham, MA: R & L Education.

Sperry, R. W. (1968). Hemisphere deconnection and unity in consciousness. *American Psychologist, 23*, 723–33.

Wagner, T. (2012). *Creating innovators: The making of young people who will change the world*. New York, NY: Simon & Schuster.

Whiteley, G. (Director). (2015). *Most likely to succeed* [Documentary]. United States: One Potato Productions.

Wiliam, D. (2011). *Embedded formative assessment: Practical strategies and tools for K–12 teachers*. Bloomington, IN: Solution Tree.

Wiliam, D. (2016). *Leadership for teacher learning: Creating a culture where all teachers improve so that all students succeed*. West Palm Beach, FL: Learning Sciences International.

Willingham, D. (2009). *Why don't students like school?: A cognitive scientist answers questions about how the mind works and what it means for the classroom*. San Francisco, CA: Jossey-Bass.

Willingham, D. (2017, May 19). You still need your brain. *New York Times*. Retrieved from https://www.nytimes.com/2017/05/19/opinion/sunday/you-still-need-your-brain.html?_r=0

Zhao, Y. (2012). *World class learners: Educating creative and entrepreneurial students*. Thousand Oaks, CA: Corwin.

Appendix

Sample Strategic Plans

Protocols

Sample Evaluation Tools

Sample Unit Plan

Demonstration Scenario

SAMPLE STRATEGIC PLANS

Sample District Action Plan 2017–2018
Serving all learners by approaching all actions with heart, mind, and action and investing in learning, teaching, and community relations.

Driving Question(s)

- *What evidence do we capture and actions do we take that enable learners to move forward in their learning?*

2017–2018 Learning Intentions
(based on Strategic Priority objectives)

(1) Learners can answer and act upon the three questions: *Where am I going?*, *Where am I?*, and *What's next?*

(2) Learners and staff work together to evaluate and take action on student progress and proficiency.

Success Criteria

- When prompted, students can answer the three questions by identifying the key learning outcome, their progress, and next steps they are taking in their learning.
- Assessment and grading practices (including report cards) enable learners to answer the three questions for all five Cs.
- Teachers work together to measure their impact, celebrate successes, and make changes that improve learning.

Key Actions (related to student learning)

- Align grading/reporting systems to best practices and research related to student performance.
- Augment district-wide assessment strategy (i.e., benchmarks) to ensure reliable and valid student performance data are captured and inform instruction and learning.
- Teach learners how to track their own progress and proficiency and discuss their learning at surface, deep, and transfer levels.

Theory of Action

If learners develop confidence in their learning, compassion for others, the knowledge and skills to collaborate, engage in creative processes to solve problems, and develop a command of academic knowledge and skills, then they will successfully continue to take action in post-[insert district name here] experiences with heart, mind, and action.

Sample Site Action Plan*

August 7, 2017:

Framing the Year

- ❑ Norms
- ❑ Pretest
- ❑ Review teacher clarity
- ❑ What are learning intentions and success criteria?
- ❑ Collective mindsets

August 17, 2017

Framing the Year

- ❑ Initiatives: Farewell
- ❑ Collaboration teams
- ❑ Write and apply learning intentions in student-friendly language that actively engages students in the learning process
- ❑ Write success criteria
- ❑ Student pre-/post-assessment
- ❑ Beginning of the year assessment
- ❑ Teachers share learning intentions and success criteria

September 14, 2017

Know Thy Impact

- ❑ Quadrants—Feedback
- ❑ So what, now what? Feedback
- ❑ Plot student success ~ analyze
- ❑ Introduce effect size spreadsheet
- ❑ Teachers share learning intentions and success criteria
- ❑ Share student focus group
- ❑ Critical Friends

*Note: The Sample Site Action Plan is courtesy of Melissa Lambert, Konocti Education (KEC), Principal, and Nichole Sabatier, KEC Assistant Principal.

Sample Site Action Plan

Yearlong Learning Progressions
Learning Intentions & Success Criteria
Goal for 2018 = One Year of Growth in One Year's Time

	October/November	December/January	Feb/March/April	May/June
Learning Intention	**First Trimester Success Criteria Checkpoint**	**Semester Success Criteria**	**Second Trimester Success Criteria Checkpoint**	**End of Year June**
To build our understanding and ability to develop quality learning intentions and success criteria, resulting in improved student outcomes	• Students can articulate what the learning intentions of a lesson are. • Students know the success criteria of a project or lesson. • Teachers collect data from assessments linked to success criteria. In reference to the above: All of our students can answer these questions, at any time, in any subject. *These questions are the focus of the instructional walkthroughs.* • Where am I going? • How do I know? • Where to next?	All teachers use success criteria clearly linked to learning intentions. Success criteria is the basis for feedback and peer/self- assessment. • **Surface:** Learning intentions and success criteria for all standards outcomes. • **Deep:** Success criteria is linked and broken into surface, deep, and transfer levels. • **Transfer:** Learners refer to success criteria to monitor growth. Learners can identify their place in learning. Transfer-level learners can give and receive feedback based on success criteria.	• Teachers initiate learners regularly, receiving feedback linked to success criteria: • So what? • Now what? • All teachers work in collaborative groups to discuss the different forms of feedback: • Proficiency vs. progress • Achievement vs. growth	All teachers use success criteria clearly linked to learning intentions. Success criteria is the basis for feedback and peer/self- assessment. • **Surface:** Learning intentions and success criteria for all standards that apply to student outcomes • **Deep:** Success criteria is linked to the learning intention and broken into surface, deep, and transfer levels. • **Transfer:** Learners refer to success criteria to monitor growth. Learners can identify their place in learning. Transfer-level learners can give and receive feedback based on success criteria.

October 12, 2017

Now What?

- ❏ Teachers share pre-/post-test of STAR
- ❏ Quadrants—feedback
- ❏ Post-assessment learning intentions and success criteria Google Form
- ❏ Admin calculate effect size
- ❏ Share student focus group
- ❏ Teachers share learning intentions and success criteria

November 9, 2017

- ❏ Admin share effect size on learning intentions and success criteria
- ❏ Teacher focus group
- ❏ Post-test student data
- ❏ Effect size entry whole group
- ❏ Quadrant analysis—Staff

January 25, 2018

So what, Now what?

- ❏ Collaborative teams
- ❏ Parent focus group
- ❏ Quadrant analysis—Students data

March 15, 2018

- ❏ Share student focus group
- ❏ Critical Friends

April 12, 2018

- ❏ Post-assessment learning intentions and success criteria Google Form
- ❏ Effect size entry whole group
- ❏ Quadrant analysis

May 10, 2018

- ❏ Celebrate!
- ❏ Letter to Self—Goals for the year

PROTOCOLS

Lead learners utilize protocols to support collective understanding, problem-solving, and decision-making. In Chapter 2, Figures 2.5 and 2.6 illustrate protocols that enable leaders to establish and clarify priorities in strategic planning. In Chapters 5 and 6, Figure 5.1 and Figure 6.3 lay out a number of protocols that support lead learners in structuring conversation and collaborative problem-solving through the CFT process. Additionally, Figure 5.8 emphasizes multiple protocols that enable leaders to structure group meetings. Several of these protocols are derived from a variety of sources including Harvey, Bearley, and Corkrum (1997), the New Tech Network, and the National School Reform Faculty.

	Protocol	**Appears in This Text**
1	Affinity Mapping	Figure 5.1, Figure 5.8
2	Boundary Setting Mission Management	Figure 5.1, Figure 5.8
3	Chalk Talk	Figure 5.1, Figure 5.8
4	Constructivist Listening	Figure 5.1, Figure 5.8
5	Constructivist Tuning Protocol	Activity 2.1, Activity 3.4, Figure 5.1, Figure 5.8
6	Consultancy Dilemma	Figure 5.1, Figure 5.8
7	Contingency Analysis	Figure 5.1
8	Cost Iceberg	Figure 5.1
9	Criteria Development	Figure 5.1, Figure 6.3
10	Critical Friends	Figure 2.5 Protocol B, Activity 2.1, Activity 3.4, Figure 5.1, Figure 5.2, Figure 5.8, Figure 5.9, Figure 6.3, Activity 6.2
11	Feedback Carousel	Figure 5.1, Figure 5.8
12	Final Word	Figure 5.1
13	Force Field Analysis	Figure 5.1
14	Future Protocol	Figure 5.1, Figure 5.8
15	Gap Analysis	Figure 5.1
16	Issaquah Protocol	Figure 5.1
17	Leadership Dilemma	Figure 5.1

	Protocol	Appears in This Text
18	Let It Go	Figure 2.5 Protocol C, Figure 5.8
19	Metaphor	Figure 5.1, Figure 6.3
20	Mind Map	Figure 5.1, Figure 6.3
21	Nominal Group Technique	Figure 5.1
22	Pareto Chart	Figure 5.1, Figure 6.3
23	Participative Management Tree	Figure 5.1
24	Personal Power Grid	Figure 5.1, Figure 6.3
25	Positive Context	Figure 5.1
26	Scenario Building	Figure 5.1
27	Snow Card	Figure 5.1
28	Stakeholder Analysis	Figure 5.1, Figure 5.8, Figure 6.3
29	SWOT Analysis	Figure 2.6, Figure 2.7, Activity 2.2, Figure 5.1, Figure 6.3
30	T-Chart	Figure 5.1, Protocol 13, Protocol 24
31	Trade-Off Analysis	Figure 5.1, Figure 5.8
32	Tree Diagram	Figure 5.1, Figure 6.3
33	What?, So What?, Now What?	Figure 2.10, Figure 5.1, Figure 6.3
34	Why Cycle	Figure 5.1
35	Zones of Comfort, Risk, and Danger	Figure 5.1, Figure 6.3

PROTOCOL 1 *AFFINITY MAPPING*

Purpose The following protocol ensures teams are synthesizing divergent or disparate information from various groups, facets of the organization, and/or external community in order to understand a problem or a solution.

Suggested Time: 45 minutes

Opening Moves (Introduction) (5 minutes)

- Review purpose of protocol.
- Review agreements (or norms) of the team.

(Continued)

(Continued)

- Identify facilitator/participant and participant.
- Review success criteria of product, process, or presentation being evaluated.

Procedure

Step 1

Hang pieces of chart paper on a wall in the room so that small groups can gather around the paper. Hand out to every participant a set of sticky notes.

Present an initial question somewhere in the room and request that participants write one idea in response to the question per sticky note. Instruct them to work silently on their own.

Step 2

Split into groups (of 4–8). In silence, put all sticky notes on designated chart paper.

Step 3

Reminding participants to remain silent, have them organize ideas by "natural" categories. Directions might sound like this:

"Which ideas go together? As long as you do not talk, feel free to move any sticky note to any place. Move yours, and those of others, and feel free to do this. Do not be offended if someone moves yours to a place that you think it does not belong; just move it to where you think it does belong—but do this all in silence."

Step 4

Once groups have settled on categories, have them place sticky notes on chart paper in designated columns. At this point, ask them to converse about the categories and come up with a name for each one.

Step 5

Have the groups pick a spokesperson to report their ideas to the larger group.

Gather that data, and have an open discussion to help participants make connections between each group's responses and categories:

1. What themes emerged? Were there any surprises?

2. What dimensions are missing from our "maps"? Again, any surprises?

3. How did this expand your knowledge or your notion of what the question at the beginning asked you to consider?

Closing Moves (5 minutes)

- Ask participants to rate how well the team executed the protocol and followed agreements.

Source: Derived from Harmony Education Center, National School Reform Faculty, 2014.

PROTOCOL 2 *BOUNDARY SETTING MISSION MANAGEMENT*

Purpose The following protocol ensures teams are focused on decisions that are aligned with the mission/vision of the organization.

Suggested Time: 45 minutes

Opening Moves (Introduction) (5 minutes)

- Review purpose of protocol.
- Review agreements (or norms) of the team.
- Identify facilitator/participant and participant.
- Review success criteria of product, process, or presentation being evaluated.

Procedure

- Identify the primary function of the department/school/district.
- Randomly interview a number of students, teachers, parents, and administrators, asking them the following question: *What is the purpose of the school or district's existence?*
- Discuss until there is a common agreement.
- Write the mission/purpose: The mission/purpose of the _____ is to ___ so that the ____students can _____

Closing Moves (5 minutes)

- Ask participants to rate how well the team executed the protocol and followed agreements.

Source: Harvey, Bearley, & Corkrum, 1997.

PROTOCOL 3 *CHALK TALK*

Purpose The following protocol ensures teams process potential problems, solutions, or implementation of solutions in a certain area of the organization.

Suggested Time: 45 minutes

Opening Moves (Introduction) (5 minutes)

- Review purpose of protocol.
- Review agreements (or norms) of the team.
- Identify facilitator/participant and participant.
- Review success criteria of product, process, or presentation being evaluated.

Procedure

Chalk Talk is a silent way to generate ideas, check on learning, develop projects, or solve problems.

Time: Varies according to need; can be from 5 minutes to an hour.
Materials: Chalkboard and chalk or paper on the wall and markers.

Process

Step 1

The facilitator explains that the chalk talk is a silent activity.

The facilitator provides materials (e.g., chalk, pens, sticky notes, large butcher paper) to groups of people.

Anyone may add to the chalk talk by writing an idea or posting a sticky note on the wall/paper/chalkboard.

Anyone may add to other people's idea by simply drawing a connecting line to the comment.

Step 2

The facilitator writes a relevant question in a circle on the board. Sample question: What are the main issues prohibiting these students from progressing?

Step 3

The facilitator states, "You may write if and when you want to. There may be long periods of silence—this is normal. Please begin."

Step 4

The facilitator may be an observer or may write questions, circle ideas, or add comments to stimulate thinking.

Step 5

At some point the activity concludes and individuals review all of the data and write down key ideas they took from the discussion. Other protocols can assist in unpacking the information.

Closing Moves (5 minutes)

- Ask participants to rate how well the team executed the protocol and followed agreements.

Source: Derived from Harmony Education Center, National School Reform Faculty, 2014.

PROTOCOL 4 *CONSTRUCTIVIST LISTENING*

Constructivist Listening

The following protocol supports group members in preparing for listening in a group setting.

Suggested Time: 10 minutes

Opening Moves (Introduction) (5 minutes)

- Review purpose of protocol.
- Review agreements (or norms) of the team.
- Identify facilitator/participant and participant.

Review Norms and Guidelines

Norm: I agree to listen and think about you in exchange for you doing the same for me.

Guidelines:

Each person

- has equal time to talk;
- does not interrupt, give advice, or break in with a personal story;
- agrees that confidentiality is maintained; and
- does not criticize or complain about others during their time to talk.

(Continued)

(Continued)

Preparation

- Facilitator asks each participant to find a partner.
- Next, the facilitator presents a prompt for each participant to share with the other (e.g., What is on top for you? What do you need to discuss to be fully present for today's work? What are you looking forward to today? What are you confused by or challenged by?).

First Cycle

- The facilitator asks the first participant to share his response with the second participant.

Second Cycle

- The facilitator states "switch" and asks the second participant to share her response with the first participant.

Closing Moves (5 minutes)

- Ask participants to rate how well the team executed the protocol and followed agreements.

Source: Derived from Harmony Education Center, National School Reform Faculty, 2014.

PROTOCOL 5 *CONSTRUCTIVIST TUNING PROTOCOL*

Purpose The following protocol provides a process for people to give and receive feedback to one another.

Suggested Time: 45 minutes

Opening Moves (Introduction) (5 minutes)

- Review purpose of protocol.
- Review agreements (or norms) of the team.

- Identify facilitator/participant and participant.
- Review success criteria of product, process, or presentation being evaluated.

Procedure

Step 1: Introduction

The facilitator states to the group that the presenter has 10 minutes to present their work to others. This is an opportunity for the participants to provide context for their work and their areas of interest for feedback. No interruptions or questions are allowed, just listening and note taking by the participants. (10 minutes)

After 10 minutes, the facilitator asks the participants if they have any clarifying questions. The facilitator typically provides 3–4 minutes for clarifying questions.

Step 2: Feedback

The facilitator thanks the presenter for presenting and then tells the presenter that they will now listen and record feedback and will not respond to any comments.

For 2 minutes, participants review their notes and collect their thoughts on feedback they can give that would be most helpful to the presenter.

Next, the facilitator asks for "Warm Feedback": Participants share the evidence they found were strengths in the presentation (5 minutes).

Next the facilitator asks for "Cool Feedback": Participants share questions that arise and feedback to move their work toward success criteria. (5 minutes)

Step 3: Next Steps

Presenter takes a few minutes to review the feedback and to consider his or her response. (2–3 minutes)

Presenter responds to those comments and questions that he or she chooses to. Participants are silent. (5 minutes)

Closing Moves (5 minutes)

- Ask participants to rate how well the team executed the protocol and followed agreements.

Source: Derived from Harmony Education Center, National School Reform Faculty, 2014.

PROTOCOL 6 *CONSULTANCY DILEMMA*

Purpose The following protocol ensures teams are thinking thoroughly through a particular situation. This protocol requires an outside entity to support the team in navigating the problem(s) successfully.

Suggested Time: 45 minutes

Opening Moves (Introduction) (5 minutes)

- Review purpose of protocol.
- Review agreements (or norms) of the team.
- Identify facilitator/team, team members, and reviewers.
- Review success criteria of product, process, or presentation being evaluated.

Procedure

Step 1: Problem Statement/Overview

A facilitator asks the presenting team or team member to provide a description of the problem they are facing. This is also a time for the presenting team or team member to share any documentation with the reviewers. (10 minutes)

Step 2: Clarifying Questions

After 10 minutes, the facilitator asks the participants if they have any clarifying questions. The facilitator typically provides 3–4 minutes for clarifying questions. The presenter may respond.

Step 3: "Priming the Pump"

For approximately 10 minutes, the group asks a series of probing questions to the team or team members to support them in thinking through their problem.

Step 4: Restating Problem Statement

The facilitator asks the team to restate the problem statement and discuss any new insights into the problem.

Step 5: Conversation

The facilitator opens the conversation up with additional questions from the reviewers to the team or team members.

Closing Moves (5 minutes)

- Ask participants to rate how well the team executed the protocol and followed agreements.

Source: Derived from Harmony Education Center, National School Reform Faculty, 2014.

PROTOCOL 7 *CONTINGENCY ANALYSIS*

Purpose The following protocol enables teams to identify specific causes, the magnitude of each cause, and potential means of prevention for specified causes to a problem.

Suggested Time: 45 minutes

Opening Moves (Introduction) (5 minutes)

- Review purpose of protocol.
- Review agreements (or norms) of the team.
- Identify facilitator/participant and participant.
- Review success criteria of product, process, or presentation being evaluated.

Procedure

- Identify the problem and record it on the top of the chart.
- Draw a diagram of a half (crescent) moon on the right side of the paper. Label the crescent with the problem.
- Draw rays "radiating" from the room. Brainstorm and identify contributing cause of the failure. Label each ray with the name of the cause. The rays indicate contributing causes of the failure.
- With each contributing cause, evaluate importance as a cause. How strong are they? What is the impact of each cause on the problem? Usually the group will use an impact scale from 1 to 10.
- Develop a checklist of preventions for each cause extending from the "ray."

Closing Moves (5 minutes)

- Ask participants to rate how well the team executed the protocol and followed agreements.

Source: Harvey, Bearley, & Corkrum, 1997.

PROTOCOL 8 *COST ICEBERG*

Purpose The following protocol enables teams to understand obvious and less obvious factors that could inhibit successful implementation of a plan.

Suggested Time: 45 minutes

Opening Moves (Introduction) (5 minutes)

- Review purpose of protocol.
- Review agreements (or norms) of the team.
- Identify facilitator/participant and participant.
- Review success criteria of product, process, or presentation being evaluated.

Procedure

- Identify the problem area.
- Label a chart with the following headings: "Overt Challenges" and "Covert Challenges."
- Each participant or team member should create a list under each heading.
- Transfer the lists on a new chart that shows an iceberg. The more overt challenges should be placed higher on the chart and the more covert challenges should be placed lower on the chart.
- Develop a plan to eliminate the challenges and bring the covert challenges to the surface.

Closing Moves (5 minutes)

- Ask participants to rate how well the team executed the protocol and followed agreements.

Source: Harvey, Bearley, & Corkrum, 1997.

PROTOCOL 9 *CRITERIA DEVELOPMENT*

Purpose The following protocol enables teams to articulate interests and share all relevant information to determine key solutions for decision-making.

Suggested Time: 30–60 minutes

Opening Moves (Introduction) (5 minutes)

- Review purpose of protocol.
- Review agreements (or norms) of the team.
- Identify facilitator/participant and participant.
- Review success criteria of product, process, or presentation being evaluated.

Procedure

- Describe needs that the problem or decision will address.
- Define the goals of the solution.
- Identify the characteristics of a solution that are essential ("needs). These characteristics must be present for the solution to be acceptable for the team. The "needs" should be posted on the wall.
- Next, discuss the characteristics for the solutions that are preferences but not essential ("want") and characteristics of a solution that would be ideal with no limitations ("nice toos").
- Through discussion, come to agreement on the criteria.
- Discuss results and decide on next steps.

Closing Moves (5 minutes)

- Ask participants to rate how well the team executed the protocol and followed agreements.

Source: Harvey, Bearley, & Corkrum, 1997.

PROTOCOL 10 *CRITICAL FRIENDS*

Purpose The following protocol is designed for providing a students and educators with specific feedback regarding a product, presentation, or process.

Suggested Time: 45 minutes

Opening Moves (Introduction) (5 minutes)

- Review purpose of protocol.
- Review agreements (or norms) of the team.

(Continued)

(Continued)

- Identify facilitator/participant and participants.
- Review success criteria of product, process, or presentation being evaluated.

Opening Presentation (5 minutes)

- The teacher or student requesting feedback provides a 10-minute overview on the product, process, or presentation.
- The facilitator will then ask the CFT for any clarifying questions.
- The presenter will provide answers to any clarifying question.

  - *This process can be much more effective when materials are provided before the CFT Review. One suggestion is to e-mail all CFT members with materials to be reviewed 72 hours before the CFT process.*

Strengths (I like) (10 minutes)

- Facilitator asks the CFT to provide feedback related to the strengths of the product, process, or presentation.
- CFT members will begin each piece of feedback using the following stems: "I like _____ because _____" or "One strength is _____ because _____." (Rationale should be related to success criteria.)

  - *During the next three sections (Strengths, Questions, and Next Steps), the teacher receiving feedback should not make any remarks and should only listen and write down notes.*
  - *The facilitator should ensure that all information is posted on the website.*

Questions (I wonder)

- Facilitator asks the CFT to provide questions for the teacher–presenter to think through the product, process, or presentation.
- CFT members will begin each piece of feedback using the following stems: "I wonder _____ because _____" or "One question to consider includes _____." (Rationale should be related to success criteria.)

Next Steps

- Facilitator asks the CFT to provide feedback related to the strengths of the product, process, or presentation.

- CFT members will begin each piece of feedback using the following stems: "I like ____ because ____" or "One strength is ____ because ____." (Rationale should be related to success criteria.)

Closing Remarks

- The teacher receiving feedback has the opportunity to thank the CFT for their feedback and to provide specific next steps they will take in light of the feedback they received.

Closing Moves (5 minutes)

- Ask participants to rate how well the team executed the protocol and followed agreements.

Source: Derived from Harmony Education Center, National School Reform Faculty, 2014.

PROTOCOL 11 *FEEDBACK CAROUSEL*

Purpose The following protocol ensures teams receive a variety of different types of feedback from a large number of people in short duration.

Suggested Time: 45 minutes

Opening Moves (Introduction) (5 minutes)

- Review purpose of protocol.
- Review agreements (or norms) of the team.
- Identify facilitator/participant and participants.
- Review success criteria of product, process, or presentation being evaluated.

Procedure

Step 1: Preparation and Presentation

The facilitator needs to prepare separate pieces of chart paper that have four quadrants. The top left quadrant is for clarifying questions, the top right quadrant is for probing questions, the third quadrant is for recommendations, and the fourth quadrant is for resources that would be useful to the planning team.

(Continued)

(Continued)

Next, the presenter presents one specific item/idea/product they want feedback on.

Step 2: Feedback

Participants offer feedback in short durations (2 minutes).

Step 3: Repeat Steps 1 and 2 with a new presenter

Closing Moves (5 minutes)

- Ask participants to rate how well the team executed the protocol and followed agreements.

Source: Derived from Harmony Education Center, National School Reform Faculty, 2014.

PROTOCOL 12 *FINAL WORD*

Purpose The following protocol ensures teams have a collective understanding of research, student work, or other written material.

Suggested Time: 45 minutes

Opening Moves (Introduction) (5 minutes)

- Review purpose of protocol.
- Review agreements (or norms) of the team.
- Identify facilitator/participant and participants.
- Review success criteria of product, process, or presentation being evaluated.

Procedure

Step 1: Preparation

Participants read a particular piece before entering the protocol.

Step 2: Starting a Round (7–10 minutes)

- Participants form groups of 4 or 5 and designate someone to start the process.

- The selected person reads a quote or makes a comment that stands out for them regarding the piece of writing. The person does not elaborate. (30–45 seconds)
- Each participant then has 60 seconds to respond to the quote or comment. No one else speaks. Once they are finished, the next person responds until it gets back to the first person that presented the quote or comment.
- The first person shares the "final word" by providing summarizing what they heard and providing a comment of their own.

Step 3: Repeating the Round

- The group then goes through the process until every participant has had a chance to provide the "final word."

Closing Moves (5 minutes)

- Ask participants to rate how well the team executed the protocol and followed agreements.

Source: Derived from Harmony Education Center, National School Reform Faculty, 2014.

PROTOCOL 13 *FORCE FIELD ANALYSIS*

Purpose The following protocol enables teams to determine forces (or factors) that enable or hinder change and identify means to move forward in the problem-solving process.

Suggested Time: 45 minutes

Opening Moves (Introduction) (5 minutes)

- Review purpose of protocol.
- Review agreements (norms) of the team.
- Identify someone as the facilitator of the process.
- Review success criteria.

Procedural Steps

- Post the following T-chart on the wall.
- Identify the ideal state (goal): *Where do we want to be?*

(Continued)

(Continued)

- Identify the current state of affairs: *Where are we now?*
- Brainstorm a series of driving and restraining forces and post on the T-chart. Once all ideas have been posted, synthesize ideas into a series of forces.
- Plot the forces on the T-chart contrasting driving forces to related restraining forces (e.g., Force #1 is inhibited or influenced by Force #6).
- Ask the group to take a few minutes to reflect on any "hidden" norms or practices that have not been mentioned as a driving or restraining force. Give people time to write a few notes and post them on the board.
- Determine the strength level of each force (1 being a low level of strength and 5 being a high level of strength).
- Post the following question: *What next steps would we need to take to reduce the restraining forces and leverage the driving forces?* Have the team discuss potential strategies and place on the bottom of the T-chart.
- Evaluate overall strategies by having participants determine whether each strategy will move the team forward (+), backwards (−), or maintain a net-neutral status (0). Each team member should mark +, −, or 0 for his or her opinion of each strategy.

Current State	Ideal State
Driving Forces (Acceleration Progress)	*Restraining Forces (Hindering Progress)*
Force #1 _____ —>	<— _____ *Force #6*
Force #2 _____ —>	<— _____ *Force #7*
Force #3 _____ —>	<— _____ *Force #8*
Force #4 _____ —>	<— _____ *Force #9*
Force #5 _____ —>	<— _____ *Force #10*
Force #1 (1——2——3——4——5)	Force #6 (1——2——3——4——5)
Force #2 (1——2——3——4——5)	Force #7 (1——2——3——4——5)
Force #3 (1——2——3——4——5)	Force #8 (1——2——3——4——5)
Force #4 (1——2——3——4——5)	Force #9 (1——2——3——4——5)
Force #5 (1——2——3——4——5)	Force #10 (1——2——3——4——5)

Strategies:

Closing Moves (5 minutes)

- Ask participants to rate how well the team executed the protocol and followed agreements.

Source: Harvey, Bearley, & Corkrum, 1997.

PROTOCOL 14 *FUTURE PROTOCOL*

Purpose The following protocol focuses groups and teams on visioning and long-term strategic planning.

Suggested Time: 45 minutes

Opening Moves (Introduction) (5 minutes)

- Review purpose of protocol.
- Review agreements (or norms) of the team.
- Identify facilitator/participant and participants.
- Review success criteria of product, process, or presentation being evaluated.

Procedure

Step 1: Presentation

Presenter presents their aspirations and intentions in the future (5–10 minutes).

Step 2: Clarifying and "Prime the Pump" Questions

Participants ask a series of questions to ensure that the presenters are clear on what outcomes they are expecting.

(Continued)

(Continued)

Step 3: Forecast

Presenters speak in present tense describing what the future looks like, feels like, and sounds like.

Step 4: Next Steps

Presenters then discuss what it looked like when the change started.

Facilitator asks participants to ask clarifying questions to ensure that presenters are concrete and explicit in their description.

Facilitators may prompt the presenters by discussing internal and external successes and challenges.

Step 5: Linkage

The facilitator then asks the presenters to discuss how they met the ideal future.

The facilitator tells participants to ask the *who, what, when, where,* and *why* questions to get to the necessary change and what was in the way (challenges) and what was a key lever (strength).

Step 6: Navigating the Journey

The facilitator puts two pieces of chart paper on the wall.

Chart I: Facilitator labels Chart I "The Journey," which includes "Ideal" on the far-right side of the paper and "Current" on the far-left side of the paper. Next, the facilitator asks participants to include all strengths and challenges that were discussed.

The presenter reviews the chart paper.

Chart II: Facilitator labels Chart II "Closing the Gap," in which participants provide suggestions on next steps.

The presenter reviews the chart paper and identifies potential next steps.

Step 7: Debrief

The presenter shares their potential next steps.

Closing Moves (5 minutes)

- Ask participants to rate how well the team executed the protocol and followed agreements.

Source: Derived from Harmony Education Center, National School Reform Faculty, 2014.

PROTOCOL 15 *GAP ANALYSIS*

The following protocol allows participants to identify the differences between the desired outcome and current performance or actual state of affairs.

Suggested Time: 35 minutes

Opening Moves (Introduction) (5 minutes)

- Review purpose of protocol.
- Review agreements (or norms) of the team.
- Identify facilitator/participant and participants.

Statements of Problem/Challenge/ Circumstance (15 minutes)

- Ask participants to identify the idea, state, or outcome they are trying to reach. Provide a scenario, review reference documents, or offer a general description.
- Ask participants to define the actual or current state/performance level at this point in time.

Next Steps (15 minutes)

- Ask participants what can be done to alleviate the discrepancy between the ideal state and current state/performance level.
- Identify five key steps the organization could take now.

Closing Moves (5 minutes)

- Ask participants to rate how well the team executed the protocol and followed agreements.

Source: Harvey, Bearley, & Corkrum, 1997.

PROTOCOL 16 *ISSAQUAH PROTOCOL*

Purpose The following protocol ensures teams are effectively supporting others in solving problems.

Suggested Time: 45 minutes

(Continued)

Opening Moves (Introduction) (5 minutes)

- Review purpose of protocol.
- Review agreements (or norms) of the team.
- Identify facilitator/participant and participants.
- Review success criteria of product, process, or presentation being evaluated.

Procedure

Step 1: Initiation

The presenter presents a concern as a question or statement.
Participants ask clarifying questions.

Step 2: Rounds

Participants form into small groups (3 or 4) and go through the following process:

1. The group collectively clarifies what they heard. Statements may include, "I heard [the presenter's name] say…" "What I'm hearing is…"

2. The group then identifies underlying assumptions or inferences they are drawing from the data. Statements may include, "What I think this means is…" or "What I think is going on in this problem is…" (Go-round, 3 minutes)

Step 3: Round Stop

After 5 minutes, the presenter listens to 60-second comments from the groups to ensure they are clear on what he or she was saying and to hear what inferences or assumptions the participants are drawing from. Question stems may include: "Are we getting it right?" or "Is what I'm/ we're saying making sense?"

The groups then ask a series of probing questions to the presenter to identify what assumptions and inferences they are operating under and whether the information from the participants is impacting their learning and whether the probing questions made him or her think differently about the dilemma or problem.

Step 4: Back to Rounds 2

Groups determine potential next steps for the presenter. Statements may include, "What if she…?" or "One thing I might consider/try/do…"

Step 5: Round Stop

After 5 minutes, the presenter listens to 60 seconds of suggestions from the group. The group then asks a series of probing questions to the presenter on potential next steps.

Closing Moves (5 minutes)

- Ask participants to rate how well the team executed the protocol and followed agreements.

Source: Derived from Harmony Education Center, National School Reform Faculty, 2014.

PROTOCOL 17 *LEADERSHIP DILEMMA*

Purpose The following protocol provides individuals with a structured process for students, teachers, and leaders to think through a challenge in a collaborative setting.

Suggested Time: 45 minutes

Opening Moves (Introduction) (5 minutes)

- Review purpose of protocol.
- Review agreements (or norms) of the team.
- Identify facilitator/presenter and reviewers.

Statements of Dilemma (10 minutes)

- The facilitator asks the presenter to present a dilemma to others. The presenter briefly explains the dilemma and addresses the following questions: *Why is this important? Why is this a dilemma? How is this a dilemma? What is causing this dilemma?* (Presenter may bring exemplars/artifacts.)
- The facilitator asks the group to provide any clarifying questions to the presenter.

Discussing Dilemma (10 minutes)

- Facilitator asks the presenter to write notes and not speak during the next 10 minutes.

(Continued)

(Continued)

- The group discusses the dilemma. The group discussion typically addresses the following questions: *What are the important facts that have emerged in this dilemma? What are the assumptions underlying the dilemma? What are potential perspectives or questions that may be of value to consider?*

Reflection From Presenter (10 minutes)

- Presenter has an opportunity to share reflections and next steps.

Reflection on Process

- The facilitator asks the presenter and the group the following questions: *What were the strengths in our adherence to the protocol? How could we improve our process?*

Closing Moves (5 minutes)

- Ask participants to rate how well the team executed the protocol and followed agreements.

Source: Derived from Harmony Education Center, National School Reform Faculty, 2014.

PROTOCOL 18 *LET IT GO*

Purpose The following protocol provides teams with a process for determining critical initiatives and eliminating or deprioritizing other initiatives.

Suggested Time: 45 minutes

Opening Moves (Introduction) (5 minutes)

- Review purpose of protocol.
- Review agreements (or norms) of the team.
- Identify facilitator/presenter and reviewers.

Procedure

- The team writes down every single initiative they are responsible for on separate sticky notes.
- The team then posts the notes on the wall in no particular order.
- The team is then tasked with categorizing the sticky notes on to the template below.
  - Columns: One side is titled "Politics of Distraction" and the other is titled "Collaborative Expertise." The facilitator may define the "Politics of Distraction" as those initiatives that promote less than one year's growth in student learning. The facilitator may define "Collaborative Expertise" as those initiatives that promote more than one year's growth in one year's time.
  - Rows: One row is titled "Within Our Control" and the other is titled "Not Within Our Control."
- Next, the team answers the following questions:
  - What initiatives in quadrant 3 are we willing to "let go" of for our students?
  - What initiatives in quadrant 1 are we willing to bring forward to others as impeding your team's ability to be successful?
  - What initiatives in quadrant 2 are you willing to continue to focus on and leverage?
  - What initiatives in quadrant 4 are we willing to bring forward to others as supporting your team's ability to be successful?
- The team determines next steps in light of these questions.

	Politics of Distraction (Less than .40 ES per year)	Collaborative Expertise (Less than .40 ES per year)
Within Our Control (of the District or School or Team)	1	2
Not Within the Control of the District or School or Team	3	4

Closing Moves (5 minutes)

Ask participants to rate how well the team executed the protocol and followed agreements.

PROTOCOL 19 *METAPHOR*

Purpose The following protocol supports teams in establishing and developing clarity during the problem-solving process.

Suggested Time: 45–60 minutes

Opening Moves (Introduction) (5 minutes)

- Review purpose of protocol.
- Review agreements (or norms) of the team.
- Identify facilitator/presenter and reviewers.

Procedure (40–50 minutes)

1. Post the problem or decision for all participants to view.

2. Ask each individual team member to draw or design (if materials are available) pictures, emblems, logos, and so on that resemble terms being discussed, the problem being solved, and the problem faced.

3. Create small teams of 2 or 3 and have members discuss their individual images.

4. Ask teams to create a collective representation that includes the multiple representations from each individual team member.

5. Have each small team share their representation.

6. Engage the larger group in what the multiple representations say about the problem/decision.

7. Determine next steps that would enable others to understand the problem/vision/terms.

Closing Moves (5 minutes)

- Ask participants to rate how well the team executed the protocol and followed agreements.

Source: Harvey, Bearley, & Corkrum, 1997.

PROTOCOL 20 *MIND MAP*

Purpose The following protocol supports teams in establishing and developing clarity of outcomes or strategy during the problem-solving process.

Suggested Time: 30–45 minutes x 2

Opening Moves (Introduction) (5 minutes)

- Review purpose of protocol.
- Review agreements (or norms) of the team.
- Identify facilitator/presenter and reviewers.

Procedure (20–35 minutes)

Part I: Divergent

- Post a large sheet of paper on the wall and provide team members with a variety of markers, colored pencils, and so on, and sticky notes with writing utensils.
- Present in the center of the paper the key problem, topic, vision, or idea.
- Ask team members to silently think about key subtopics (key ideas, activities, resources, steps) that would relate with the main topic.
- Have team members write down ideas for subtopics on sticky notes on the large sheet of paper. During this time, all participants should begin silently categorizing sticky notes in groups around the central theme.
- Next, assign a subtopic to each group and have each group begin developing symbols, graphics, stories, and so on to that subtopic.
- Next, have each group review all subtopics and discuss as a team, asking clarifying questions and building upon what others have written.
- Take a picture and post online for the teams to review and/or post in a collaborative space.

Part II: Convergent

- Have each team member rate his or her level of understanding of the problem, on a scale of 1–5.

(Continued)

(Continued)

- Based on the score, have small teams review the central topic, sub-topics, and steps included on the mind map. During this review, teams should answer the following questions:

  ○ Do we know where we are going?

    ▪ Do we know the key outcomes?
    ▪ Do we know the boundaries of the decision-making process?

  ○ Do we know where we are?

    ▪ Have we shared all relevant information? Who is not at the table?
    ▪ Do we understand what key terms mean and processes included on the topic?

  ○ What's next?

    ▪ Given our mind map, what steps do you suggest we take?

- As a larger team, work together to go through the three key questions and determine if (a) support is needed to establish clarity, (b) a greater level of involvement is necessary, and/or (c) there is a collective interest in a particular approach for moving forward.

Closing Moves (5 minutes)

- Ask participants to rate how well the team executed the protocol and followed agreements.

Source: Harvey, Bearley, & Corkrum, 1997.

PROTOCOL 21 *NOMINAL GROUP TECHNIQUE*

Purpose The following protocol promotes divergent and convergent idea generation and clarification.

Suggested Time: 45 minutes

Opening Moves (Introduction) (5 minutes)

- Review purpose of protocol.
- Review agreements (or norms) of the team.
- Identify facilitator/presenter and reviewers.

Procedure

- Present the problem or decision.
- Tell the large group or staff that they will have a few minutes to think about the problem.
- Form teams (3 or 4) and have the team members generate and write their ideas on a notecard (they could prepare these before everyone meets).
- Gather ideas from each of the individuals in a round-robin style and record them on a chart.
- When all of the ideas have been recorded, the group then discusses each idea in order to be sure that everyone has a common understanding of each idea. If the group is large, put the members into smaller groups to collaborate and collectively share information, merits, and demerits of each idea.
- With the group's agreements, eliminate duplicate ideas and combine similar ones.

Closing Moves (5 minutes)

- Ask participants to rate how well the team executed the protocol and followed agreements.

Source: Harvey, Bearley, & Corkrum, 1997.

PROTOCOL 22 *PARETO CHART*

Purpose The following protocol enables teams to identify problems that cause the greatest level of challenge for an organization.

Suggested Time: 45 minutes

Opening Moves (Introduction) (5 minutes)

- Review purpose of protocol.
- Review agreements (or norms) of the team.
- Identify facilitator/participant and participants.
- Review success criteria of product, process, or presentation being evaluated.

(Continued)

(Continued)

Procedure

- Select a problem in which the causes or possible subproblems can be quantified and turned into percentages.
- Identify each cause or subproblem.
- Collect data on the occurrence of each cause or subproblem.
- Draw a vertical line for the y-axis and connected horizontal line for the x-axis.
- Put the frequency, quantity, or occurrences along the y-axis and the labels for the categories along the x-axis to the right.
- Draw a bar the height of which matches the frequencies on the y-axis to the left for each cause or subproblem.
- Calculate a percentage of the total represented by each cause or subproblem. Draw a cumulative percentage line starting in the lower-left corner at 0 percent. Place a dot above each bar showing the cumulative percentage to that bar. Connect the dots to make the cumulative-percentage line.
- Use the 80/20 principle to select the causes or subproblem that will you give you the biggest payoff.

Closing Moves (5 minutes)

- Ask participants to rate how well the team executed the protocol and followed agreements.

Source: Harvey, Bearley, & Corkrum, 1997.

PROTOCOL 23 *PARTICIPATIVE MANAGEMENT TREE*

Purpose The following protocol enables groups/teams to identify the most appropriate means for selecting a decision-making process for problems.

Suggested Time: 45 minutes

Opening Moves (Introduction) (5 minutes)

- Review purpose of protocol.
- Review agreements (or norms) of the team.
- Identify facilitator/participant and participants.
- Review success criteria of product, process, or presentation being evaluated.

Procedure

- Show the group/team four decision-making processes:

Consultation	Command	Consensus	Convenience
• Leader gets information/ input from others before making an individual decision.	• Leaders make the decision without input.	• Leaders make the decision with a majority of agreement and no serious disagreement.	• Leaders allocate decision-making to whatever makes the most sense.

- Clearly identify the decision or problem situation.
- Move through the tree below, starting at the far left. Do this by answering questions 1–5 as indicated by the tree. These questions relate to the considerations of time, trust, teamwork, importance, and acceptance.

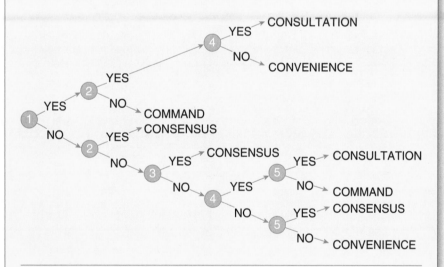

Source: Harvey, Bearley, & Corkrum, 1997, p. 190.

Closing Moves (5 minutes)

- Ask participants to rate how well the team executed the protocol and followed agreements.

PROTOCOL 24 *PERSONAL POWER GRID*

Purpose The following protocol allows individual group members and the collective to articulate perceived "power" over a decision/process/problem.

Suggested Time: 45 minutes

Opening Moves (Introduction) (5 minutes)

- Review purpose of protocol.
- Review agreements (or norms) of the team.
- Identify facilitator/participant and participant.
- Review success criteria of product, process, or presentation being evaluated.

Procedure

- Identify the key area of focus (i.e., specific decision/problem/process).
- Create a T-chart and write as a header on one side "Outside of Our Control" and on the other write "Within Our Control."
- Develop a list, via brainstorming sticky notes under each category on the T-chart.
- Categorize the list of sticky notes under each category on the T-chart.
- Discuss how the group/team can or cannot influence each column.
- Utilize the list during problem-solving meetings.

Closing Moves (5 minutes)

- Ask participants to rate how well the team executed the protocol and followed agreements.

Source: Harvey, Bearley, & Corkrum, 1997.

PROTOCOL 25 *POSITIVE CONTEXT*

Purpose The following protocol supports teams in developing processes for improving team dynamics.

Suggested Time: 45 minutes

Opening Moves (Introduction) (5 minutes)

- Review purpose of protocol.
- Review agreements (or norms) of the team.
- Identify facilitator/presenter and reviewers.

Procedure

- Ask participants to describe beliefs, behaviors, or conditions in the past that were helpful in effective decision-making. List on chart paper.
- Ask participants to describe beliefs, behaviors, or conditions in the past that were inhibited in effective decision-making. List on chart paper.
- Discuss the key positive and negative beliefs, behaviors, or conditions that were most important.
- Write down (e.g., draw arrows connecting) the relationship between positive and negative beliefs, behaviors, or conditions.
- Utilize the positive elements as part of constructing norms/agreements and as a way to review norms before each meeting and to discuss approaches for intervening when negative behaviors are expressed in meetings.

Closing Moves (5 minutes)

- Ask participants to rate how well the team executed the protocol and followed agreements.

Source: Harvey, Bearley, & Corkrum, 1997.

PROTOCOL 26 *SCENARIO BUILDING*

Purpose The following protocol supports teams in analyzing information through storytelling.

Suggested Time: 45 minutes

Opening Moves (Introduction) (5 minutes)

- Review purpose of protocol.
- Review agreements (or norms) of the team.
- Identify facilitator/presenter and reviewers.

Procedure

- Pick a particular future time and setting that is appropriate to the decision (e.g., what student learning looks like in 5 years).

(Continued)

(Continued)

- Ask participants to write a story for that setting.
- Ask participants to share stories in total group or in a subgroup if the group is large.
- Have participants discuss their stories about organizational changes and needs.

Closing Moves (5 minutes)

- Ask participants to rate how well the team executed the protocol and followed agreements.

Source: Harvey, Bearley, & Corkrum, 1997.

PROTOCOL 27 *SNOW CARD*

Purpose The following protocol enables teams to develop and understand key solution criteria, clarify similarities and differences between solution choices, and generate potential solutions in the decision-making process.

Suggested Time: 90 minutes

Opening Moves (Introduction) (5 minutes)

- Review purpose of protocol.
- Review agreements (or norms) of the team.
- Identify facilitator/presenter and reviewers.

Procedure

- Present the key decision situation.
- Give each team member a series of sticky notes. Instruct each person to write one response per notecard.
- Post the notecards of the wall.
- Read the ideas on the cards and ask for clarification.
- Group sticky notes based on similarities of ideas.
- The idea that has the most notecards become a starting point for discussions within teams or the larger group.
- Discuss areas to reach consensus.

Closing Moves (5 minutes)

- Ask participants to rate how well the team executed the protocol and followed agreements.

Source: Derived from Harmony Education Center, National School Reform Faculty, 2014.

PROTOCOL 28 *STAKEHOLDER ANALYSIS*

Purpose The following protocol enables teams to identify key stakeholders and their level of influence and involvement in problems, opportunities, and processes.

Suggested Time: 90 minutes

Opening Moves (Introduction) (5 minutes)

- Review purpose of protocol.
- Review agreements (or norms) of the team.
- Identify facilitator/presenter and reviewers.

Procedure

- Present the following chart to the group/team:

Problem/Decision/Process:

Internal Stakeholders DOS	External Stakeholders DOS

DOS (degree of stakeholding): How important are the results of this problem/decision/process to individual/group, using a scale of 1 to 10, with 1 = minimal importance and 10 = maximum importance?

- Ask participants to identify internal and external stakeholders that have a stake in the problem/decision/process.

(Continued)

(Continued)

- Rate the "Degree of Stakeholding" (DOS) using a 1–10 scale (with 1 = minimal importance and 10 = maximum importance).
- Discuss level of involvement for each stakeholder group and create next steps. Results above 6 should be routinely involved, 3–5 should be infrequently involved, and a 1–2 have relatively little importance in being involved.

Closing Moves (5 minutes)

- Ask participants to rate how well the team executed the protocol and followed agreements.

Source: Harvey, Bearley, & Corkrum, 1997.

PROTOCOL 29 *SWOT ANALYSIS*

Purpose The following protocol allows participants to evaluate strengths, weaknesses, opportunities, and threats that are critical for analyzing internal and external constraints.

Suggested Time: 45 minutes

Opening Moves (Introduction) (5 minutes)

- Review purpose of protocol.
- Review agreements (or norms) of the team.
- Identify facilitator/participant and participants.
- Post chart and label with the following words: "Strengths," "Weaknesses," "Opportunities," and "Threats." See the figure below for an exemplar.

Strengths	Weaknesses
Opportunities	Threats

Statements of Problem/Challenge/ Circumstance (10 minutes)

- Present the idea/challenge or circumstance.
- Discuss the need to identify potential strengths/weaknesses/ opportunities/threats.
- Participants should form into small groups of 3 or 4.

Group Development (10 minutes)

- Groups begin developing ideas (typically on sticky notes) and including them under each of the four quadrants of the matrix.

Collective Group Discussion (10 minutes)

- Everyone comes back and discusses the following questions:
  - What key ideas stand out? What surprises you?
  - What inferences emerge? What themes and patterns emerge? What implications to our organization can we draw?
  - What can we do with this information? What next steps do you recommend?

Moves (5 minutes)

- Ask participants to rate how well the team executed the protocol and followed agreements.

Source: Harvey, Bearley, & Corkrum, 1997.

PROTOCOL 30 *T-CHART*

Purpose The following protocol supports teams in defining problems and exploring alternatives.

Suggested Time: 45 minutes

(Continued)

(Continued)

Opening Moves (Introduction) (5 minutes)

- Review purpose of protocol.
- Review agreements (or norms) of the team.
- Identify facilitator/presenter and reviewers.

Procedure

- Create several T-charts.

  ○ Draw a horizontal line across the top of a piece of chart paper.
  ○ Draw a vertical line from the center of the horizontal line.

- Assign participants into smaller teams to review each T-chart and answer a key question: _____
- Each team should brainstorm ideas on their respective T-chart.
- After 10 minutes, each team should rotate to other groups and review each list.
- Finally, the entire group should discuss similarities and differences from the group, discuss next steps, and talk about potential implications for the organization.

Closing Moves (5 minutes)

- Ask participants to rate how well the team executed the protocol and followed agreements.

Source: Harvey, Bearley, & Corkrum, 1997.

PROTOCOL 31 *TRADE-OFF ANALYSIS*

Purpose The following protocol enables groups and teams to analyze the importance and efficacy of potential solutions.

Suggested Time: 45 minutes

Opening Moves (Introduction) (5 minutes)

- Review purpose of protocol.
- Review agreements (or norms) of the team.

- Identify facilitator/participant and participants.
- Review success criteria of product, process, or presentation being evaluated.

Procedure

- Provide solution criteria to the entire group/team.
- List potential solutions.
- Create a numerical weight for each solution criteria ("needs" should have a higher weight than "wants" and "nice toos"; "wants" should have higher weight than "nice toos" criteria).
- Have the group divide into small subgroups of 2 or 3 and score each potential solution relative to the solution criteria.
- Each group should share their score and ranking of each solution.
- Engage in a discussion of potential next steps with the larger group.

Closing Moves (5 minutes)

- Ask participants to rate how well the team executed the protocol and followed agreements.

Source: Harvey, Bearley, & Corkrum, 1997.

PROTOCOL 32 *TREE DIAGRAM*

Purpose The following protocol enables teams to understand the relationship between factors that influence (and cause) problems.

Suggested Time: 45 minutes

Opening Moves (Introduction) (5 minutes)

- Review purpose of protocol.
- Review agreements (or norms) of the team.
- Identify facilitator/participant and participants.
- Review success criteria of product, process, or presentation being evaluated.

(Continued)

(Continued)

Procedure

- Construct a tree trunk (with branches) on a sheet of paper or whiteboard for the team.
- Provide sticky notes to each team member and ask them to write down the causes of the problem or opportunity (5 minutes).
- Tell the participants to stick the sticky notes on the trunk of the tree in the front of the room.
- Number each note and have the group categorize common themes.
- Organize and line up the causes in order of sequence and determine main causes.
- Transfer the "main" causes to the "tree" (as if they were limbs extending from the trunk). Note the numbers of individual items that comprise the category.
- For each main cause, ask "Why is this happening?" These become subcauses.
- Post the subcauses under the main cause as smaller "limbs."
- Review and discuss each major cause category.
- Ask, "Why (is this a cause)?" Record responses.
- Use the Why Cycle to get to the root cause and repeatedly ask "Why?"
- Agree on causes.
- When completed, reflect on visual display and decide on next steps.

The "trunk" messages indicate individual estimates of causes. The limbs represent the grouped causes. For example, work conditions is the overall category for item 2 and 3 on the trunk.

Closing Moves (5 minutes)

- Ask participants to rate how well the team executed the protocol and followed agreements.

Source: Harvey, Bearley, & Corkrum, 1997.

PROTOCOL 33 *WHAT?, SO WHAT?, NOW WHAT?*

Purpose The following protocol allows participants to separate observations and facts from inferences/assumptions in order to make effective individual and collective decisions.

Suggest Time: 45 minutes

Opening Moves (Introduction) (5 minutes)

- Review purpose of protocol.
- Review agreements (or norms) of the team.
- Identify facilitator/participant and participants.

Statements of Problem/Challenge/ Circumstance (10 minutes)

- The facilitator asks a participant to outline a current challenge/ problem/or circumstance.
- The facilitator asks for clarifying questions from other participants.
- The facilitator then asks everyone to identify the facts of the challenge/problem/circumstance. (What do we know are facts from this challenge?)
- The facilitator populates that information onto a chart under the term "What?"

Mastering Our Stories—*So What?* (10 minutes)

- The facilitator then asks what appear to be inferences/assumptions that are drawn from the challenge. (What are we assuming or taking for granted? What other assumptions may there be?) The facilitator populates this information onto a chart under the term "So What?"
- The facilitator asks the participants to consider all of the people who are impacted by this challenge and identify what assumptions they may possess in this challenge.

Taking Action—*Now What?* (10 minutes)

- Next, the facilitator asks each participant to write down three or four specific next steps on sticky notes. The facilitator provides the following prompts: What additional information do we need? What assumptions do we need to check? What appear to be logical next steps in moving toward a solution?
- The facilitator asks the participants to silently place their sticky notes under a column entitled "Next Steps." Participants may group the sticky notes quietly.
- The facilitator then asks the group to describe the groupings. (What appear to be the major themes related to next steps?)
- The facilitator asks the original participant if he or she would like to share next steps he or she is considering.

(Continued)

(Continued)

- The facilitator then asks the original participant when he or she should check back on action steps and outcomes.
- The session is then closed.

Closing Moves (5 minutes)

- Ask participants to rate how well the team executed the protocol and followed agreements.

Source: Derived from Harmony Education Center, National School Reform Faculty, 2014.

PROTOCOL 34 *WHY CYCLE*

Purpose The following protocol enables team to understand the root causes of a problem.

Suggested Time: 45 minutes

Opening Moves (Introduction) (5 minutes)

- Review purpose of protocol.
- Review agreements (or norms) of the team.
- Identify facilitator/participant and participants.
- Review success criteria of product, process, or presentation being evaluated.

Purpose

- Present problem or decision.
- Identify causes (as currently presented).
- Ask the group to address the following question: *Why is this a cause?*
- Record responses to the question.
- Repeat the question four more times and record responses.
- Ask the group if the root cause has been identified.

Closing Moves (5 minutes)

- Ask participants to rate how well the team executed the protocol and followed agreements.

Source: Derived from Harmony Education Center, National School Reform Faculty, 2014.

PROTOCOL 35 *ZONES OF COMFORT, RISK, AND DANGER*

Purpose The following protocol ensures teams are emotionally prepared to engage in a cognitively challenging task.

Suggested Time: 45 minutes

Opening Moves (Introduction) (5 minutes)

- Review purpose of protocol.
- Review agreements (or norms) of the team.
- Identify facilitator/participant and participants.
- Review success criteria of product, process, or presentation being evaluated.

Procedure

- The facilitator brings a scenario forward to the team (usually this is brought forward by the team earlier).
- The facilitator has the team draw three concentric circles on a sheet of paper. The middle circle is labeled "Comfort," the second is labeled "Risk," and the third is labeled "Danger."
- The facilitator states to the team that the size of each circle should be correlated to the amount of time, energy, and effort that is faced in that zone. If needed, the facilitator will define the terms (comfort: feels safe and no learning is happening; risk: feels safe and feels challenged cognitively in learning; danger: feels unsafe emotionally and unable to learn or face challenges).
- The facilitator then asks the team to review their map and discuss their scenario and why they drew the map the way they did.
- Engage in constructivist listening between pairs.
- The facilitator asks the groups to engage in a learning dilemma.
- The facilitator then asks the group to identify potential next steps.

Closing Moves (5 minutes)

- Ask participants to rate how well the team executed the protocol and followed agreements.

Source: Derived from Harmony Education Center, National School Reform Faculty, 2014.

SAMPLE EVALUATION TOOLS

The following tools illustrate an approach for determining beliefs and behaviors in the classroom. These tools may be used as a means of discussing a teacher's impact on student learning, expectations of students' ability to learn, and determining potential next steps for moving student learning forward.

Student Survey—Grades 3–8 Instructions Thank you for taking this survey. Please answer honestly. Fill in one (1) circle per question. Fill in the circle like this: ● **Example:** My teacher challenges me.	Strongly Disagree ○	Disagree ○	Agree ●	Strongly Agree ○
1. My teacher often checks whether I'm understanding the work.	○	○	○	○
2. My teacher helps me achieve things I didn't think I could.	○	○	○	○
3. My teacher thinks that everyone can learn.	○	○	○	○
4. My teacher helps me with my learning.	○	○	○	○
5. My teacher understands where I'm at with my learning.	○	○	○	○
6. My teacher helps me at the right level for me.	○	○	○	○
7. My teacher has conversations with me.	○	○	○	○
8. My teacher challenges me.	○	○	○	○
9. My teacher gives me time to figure things out.	○	○	○	○
10. My teacher often gives me feedback about my work.	○	○	○	○
11. I trust my teacher.	○	○	○	○
12. It's OK to make mistakes in this teacher's class.	○	○	○	○
13. My teacher helps me understand how to learn.	○	○	○	○
14. My teacher encourages me to concentrate and stick to things even when it is hard.	○	○	○	○

Student Survey—Grades 3–8 <u>Instructions</u> Thank you for taking this survey. Please answer honestly. Fill in one (1) circle per question. Fill in the circle like this: ● **Example:** My teacher challenges me.	Strongly Disagree ○ ☹	Disagree ○ ☹	Agree ● ☺	Strongly Agree ○ ☺
15. My teacher explains what I'm learning and why.	○	○	○	○
16. My teacher gives clear instructions that are easy to follow.	○	○	○	○
17. My teacher gives me choices in how I show my learning and what I am learning.	○	○	○	○

Teacher: _____

Grade/Subject Matter: Date: Time:

How do students demonstrate that they are clear about what they are learning and what success looks like?

Do the students know where they are going? Where they are now? And what steps do they need to take to move forward in their learning?

Who does the talking? What is the balance between teacher talk and student talk?

Which students are actively supporting one another in learning? What evidence do you have to back up that assertion?

What feedback do I provide the students? What do they do with that feedback?

Have I used a range of instructional strategies?

Which students are engaged in the lesson? Which are not? Why?

How do I communicate high expectations to learners?

What is the nature of the questions (surface or deep)?

Is the classroom managed effectively? What evidence do I have to back my assertion?

Other comments:

Teacher:

Grade Level: Date: Time:

	Class 1	Class 2	Class 3	Class 4	Class 5	Class 6	%
Date							
Time							
How many in this class?							
What time into the lesson?							
Beginning							
Middle							
End							
What are the students doing?							
Listening to teacher							
Reading							
Active							

Observation Notes

Do the students know where they are going? Are students able to articulate what success looks like?

Where they are now? And what steps do they need to take to move forward in their learning?

What is the balance of dialogue and monologue in the classroom?

How are students supporting each other in the learning process?

What instructional strategies are evident? How are those instructional strategies eliciting evidence of learning? How is that evidence being used in the classroom?

What evidence is available to indicate the classroom is managed effectively?

What evidence is available to indicate that students are engaged in their learning?

```



```

What evidence is available to indicate assessment data are utilized to inform instruction? What evidence is available to indicate that students are using feedback given from the teacher, peers, or through self-assessment?

```



```

Other comments:

```



```

Signature of teacher: _____ Date:_____

Signature and title of evaluator: _____ Date:_____

It is understood that in signing this form, the teacher acknowledges having seen and discussed the report. The teacher's signature does not necessarily imply agreement with the conclusion of the report. If he or she desires, the teacher may attach a written statement.

SAMPLE UNIT PLAN

Dear Students,

The Fort Ross Conservancy, in partnership with the Russian and United States governments, are identifying weighing the benefits and challenges of reintroducing the California Sea Otter to the Northern Coast of California near Fort Ross. As a means to develop community awareness for this issue and potentially re-establish an eradicated species from its ecosystem, the Fort Ross Conservancy is seeking out your support! Specifically, the Russian and U.S. governments are equally sensitive to their partnership in this work and believe that having students identify potential next steps will lead to a greater level of "buy-in" from their respective citizens in this idea.

Your task is to design and present a solution to your local community on whether reintroduction is necessary in Fort Ross, California. This presentation should include historical information on how the sea otter was removed in the first place, the biological implications of the removal and reintroduction of species, and how reintroduction would or would not be a benefit to the ecosystem. As with all of our work, your presentation should be anchored by a descriptive essay detailing the major biological implications of reintroduction and removal of a species. We expect a detailed account of how producers, consumers, and decomposers within food chains and food webs may be impacted by our decisions. In addition, community members will be interested to know how they can "lend a hand" to support your recommendations.

We thank you for your consideration of this task and, if accepted, request that your presentation and feedback from the community be conducted within the next six weeks.

Kind Regards,

Fort Ross Conservancy Staff

Project Design From Russia With Love

Step 1: Learning Intention(s)

	I will develop a model to describe the movement of matter among plants, animals, decomposers, and the environment.

Step 2: Success Criteria

	Surface	Deep	Transfer
	Students will . . .	Students will . . .	Students will . . .
	• Define food chains, food webs, ecosystems • Describe a healthy ecosystem • List types of organisms (producers, consumers, decomposers) • Describe introduction and reintroduction of a species	• Relate food chains and food webs • Relate types of organisms and their role in food chains and food webs • Relate introduction or reintroduction to the balance of ecosystems • Relate the complexity of food chains/webs to the health of an ecosystem	• Apply the conception of reintroduction to the health of an ecosystem into unique contexts • Hypothesize the impact of potential solutions to the reintroduction or removal of species on plants, animals, and humans

Step 3: Driving Question(s)

	How do we ensure that ecosystems remain healthy when a species is reintroduced?

Context	Sea otters Wolves Elephants

Project Design From Russia With Love

Step 4: Tasks

	Surface	Deep	Transfer
	• Define terms and concepts related to food chains, food webs, and introduction/reintroduction of species • Create an outline for descriptive essay	• Build a graphic organizer that illustrates the relationship between food chains and food webs • Complete lab that illustrates transfer of energy • Develop descriptive essay that includes "what makes good writing"	• Present solution to the driving questions • Collaborate with others to design solutions across various contexts

Step 5: Entry Event

Scenario: Reintroduction of species

Expectations: Presentation/essay

Patron: Fort Ross Conservancy

Format: Written document

Workshops

	Surface	Deep	Transfer
	Workshop 1: Jigsaw elements Workshop 2: Lab Workshop 3: "Descriptive Essay WMG"	Workshop 4: Concept mapping Workshop 5: Lab Workshop 6: Peer feedback on "Descriptive Essay WMG"	Workshop 7: Comparing and contrasting changes in ecosystems

Project Design From Russia With Love

Project Calendar

	Monday	Tuesday	Wednesday	Thursday	Friday
Week 1 *[Phase 1 and Phase 2]*	Provide entry event Know/Need to Know Pre-assessment	Review Know/Need to Know Workshop (1)	Review Know/Need to Know Workshop (1)	Review Know/Need to Know Workshop (3)	Review Know/Need to Know Workshop (4)
Week 2 *[Phase 2 and Phase 3]*	Review Know/Need to Know Workshop (5)	Review Know/Need to Know Workshop (6)	Review Know/Need to Know Workshop (6)	Post-assessment	Review Know/Need to Know Form Groups Workshop (7)
Week 3 *[Phase 3 and Phase 4]*	Review Know/Need to Know Workshop (7)	Prepare for presentation	Presentation	Problem-solving task (new context) New Groups	Debrief

DEMONSTRATION SCENARIO

You have received pre-/post-test results from your learners. You still have a week to support your learners before you need to move on. What do you notice? What inferences do you draw? What next steps would you take?

Index

CORWIN

A SAGE Publishing Company

Helping educators make the greatest impact

CORWIN HAS ONE MISSION: to enhance education through intentional professional learning.

We build long-term relationships with our authors, educators, clients, and associations who partner with us to develop and continuously improve the best evidence-based practices that establish and support lifelong learning.

CORWIN LEADERSHIP

Anthony Kim & Alexis Gonzales-Black
Designed to foster flexibility and continuous innovation, this resource expands cutting-edge management and organizational techniques to empower schools with the agility and responsiveness vital to their new environment.

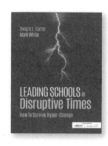

Jonathan Eckert
Explore the collective and reflective approach to progress, process, and programs that will build conditions that lead to strong leadership and teaching, which will improve student outcomes.

PJ Caposey
Offering a fresh perspective on teacher evaluation, this book guides administrators to transform their school culture and evaluation process to improve teacher practice and, ultimately, student achievement.

Dwight L. Carter & Mark White
Through understanding the past and envisioning the future, the authors use practical exercises and real-life examples to draw the blueprint for adapting schools to the age of hyper-change.

Raymond L. Smith & Julie R. Smith
This solid, sustainable, and laser-sharp focus on instructional leadership strategies for coaching might just be your most impactful investment toward student achievement.

Simon T. Bailey & Marceta F. Reilly
This engaging resource provides a simple, sustainable framework that will help you move your school from mediocrity to brilliance.

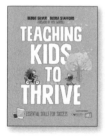

Debbie Silver & Dedra Stafford
Equip educators to develop resilient and mindful learners primed for academic growth and personal success.

Peter Gamwell & Jane Daly
Discover a new perspective on how to nurture creativity, innovation, leadership, and engagement.

To order your copies, visit **corwin.com/leadership**

Leadership That Makes an Impact

Steven Katz, Lisa Ain Dack, & John Malloy

Leverage the oppositional forces of top-down expectations and bottom-up experience to create an intelligent, responsive school.

Peter M. DeWitt

Centered on staff efficacy, these resources present discussion questions, vignettes, strategies, and action steps to improve school climate, leadership collaboration, and student growth.

Eric Sheninger

Harness digital resources to create a new school culture, increase communication and student engagement, facilitate real-time professional growth, and access new opportunities for your school.

Russell J. Quaglia, Kristine Fox, Deborah Young, Michael J. Corso, & Lisa L. Lande

Listen to your school's voice to see how you can increase engagement, involvement, and academic motivation.

Michael Fullan, Joanne Quinn, & Joanne McEachen

Learn the right drivers to mobilize complex, coherent, whole-system change and transform learning for all students.

CORWIN LEADERSHIP